The

California
Criminal Justice System

THE CALIFORNIA CRIMINAL JUSTICE SYSTEM

JAMES R. LASLEY, Ph.D
California State University, Fullerton

MICHAEL HOOPER, Ph.D
Pennsylvania State University, Harrisburg

with

GEORGE M. DERY, III, J.D
California State University, Fullerton

Production Supervisor: *Mary Carnis*
Acquisitions Editor: *Neil Marquardt*
Director of Production: *Bruce Johnson*
Production Manager: *Ed O'Dougherty*
Production Editors: *Denise Brown*

A Simon & Schuster Company
Upper Saddle River, New Jersey 07458

Printed in the United States of America
10 9 8 7 6 5 4 3

ISBN 0-13-571522-9

Prentice-Hall International (UK) Limited, *London*
Prentice-Hall of Australia Pty. Limited, *Sydney*
Prentice-Hall Canada Inc., *Toronto*
Prentice-Hall Hispanoamericana, S.A., *Mexico*
Prentice-Hall of India Private Limited, *New Delhi*
Prentice-Hall of Japan, Inc., *Tokyo*
Simon & Schuster Asia Pte. Ltd., *Singapore*
Editora Prentice-Hall do Brasil, Ltda., *Rio de Janeiro*

CONTENTS

Acknowledgements

The authors would like to express their sincere thanks to the following individuals for their assistance in the preparation of this book:

- Detective Tony Sanchez, Los Angeles Police Department
- Alan Deal, Senior Consultant, California Commission on Peace Officer Standards and Training
- Susan Haake, Senior Librarian, California Commission on Peace Officer Standards and Training
- Bruce Ward, Deputy Director, California Office of Emergency Services
- Gil Enriquez, Enriquez Bail Bonds, West Covina, CA
- Kathryn Lasley, Chino Unified School District
- Sgt. Bob Fitzer, San Francisco Police Department
- Randel R. Niznik, DPO, Orange County Probation Department

1.1

A BRIEF HISTORY OF CALIFORNIA POLICING

THE DEVELOPMENT OF CALIFORNIA POLICE

The pattern for the present-day policing of California began to take shape at the beginning of the 20th Century. Prior to 1900 the sheriffs, city marshals, and the few city-organized police departments had performed the police functions. San Francisco organized the state's first law enforcement body that functioned in the American tradition of policing in 1847, three years before statehood was achieved in California. The city of Los Angeles elected its first city marshal in 1850 and in 1869 organized the Los Angeles Police Department.[1]

California has had a profound influence on the evolution of contemporary law enforcement. The influence of California policing practices on policing nationally has been unsurpassed by any other state. From the 1920s onward, California police departments have been in the forefront of police reform.[2]

August Vollmer: Californian & The Father of Police Professionalism

The image of policing as known today is largely the creation of one man, August Vollmer.[3] In 1905 Vollmer began his law enforcement career as the elected town marshal of Berkeley, California. In 1909, after a municipal reorganization, Vollmer was appointed Chief of Police of Berkeley and held that office until his retirement in 1932.

Vollmer's most lasting contributions began in 1914 when he introduced the first automobile patrol service in American policing.[4] Two years later at the University of California at Berkeley Vollmer established a law enforcement training program, which over the next several decades was copied in whole or large part by police agencies both within and outside the United States.[5] Also in 1916 Vollmer created the first scientific crime laboratory in the country. Within a span of six years, both the first lie detector to be used in criminal investigation and a single-fingerprint classification system emerged as innovative products of the crime laboratory.[6]

Vollmer's influence, particularly his belief in the value of college education for police officers, spread throughout California. In the summer of 1918 the University of California at Los Angeles offered a program in criminology for policewomen. In 1923 a "first" was recorded when the University of California at Berkeley awarded a baccalaureate degree to a police officer with a minor in criminology.[7] In 1930 the first two-year college police program in the United States was established at San Jose Junior College.[8]

INCREASING PROFESSIONALISM

The Wickersham Commission and Vollmer's Reforms

The 1930s became a pivotal period as American police gained increasing legitimacy and authority in society. Starting in 1931, the National Commission on Law Observance and Enforcement, popularly named the "Wickersham Commission," promulgated a number of reforms for the police. Central to the Commission's recommendations were provisions for civil service status for police and enhanced support for education and training, issues identified by August Vollmer in his Report on Police for the Commission.[9] California higher education institutions spearheaded implementation of the Wickersham Commission recommendations by establishing a number of new police educational programs. Los Angeles City College and the University of Southern California offered specialized law enforcement programs in 1932 and 1933, respectively. Also, in 1935 San Jose State Teachers College gained authorization to grant a baccalaureate degree for a law enforcement major.[10]

After his retirement as police chief in 1932, Vollmer accepted an appointment as a professor of police administration in the Political Science Department of the University of California at Berkeley and worked with Professor A.M. Kidd on establishing a criminology curriculum which many years later, in the 1950s, emerged as the first school of criminology in an American university. Subsequently, Vollmer founded the American Society of Criminology, which continues to be a prestigious national (and international) association of scholars and practitioners dedicated to the advancement of criminological knowledge.[11]

O. W. Wilson: Police Administration Pioneer

Interestingly, the other figure who made a significant impression on contemporary policing in America was also a Californian. During the last half of the 20th Century, the name "O.W. Wilson" (Orlando Winfield Wilson) had become synonymous with professional police administration practices. Wilson enrolled at the University of California at Berkeley in 1920. While a student at Berkeley, Wilson was attracted by a campus newspaper ad, placed by Vollmer, to join the Berkeley Police Department. When he completed his university studies in 1924, Wilson was positioned by Vollmer as a candidate for the Chief of Police position at the Fullerton, California, Police Department. Wilson proved successful in his quest. He subsequently became the Chief of Police of the Wichita, Kansas, Police Department.

Following his service during World War II, Wilson taught at the University of California at Berkeley. He became the first Dean of the School of Criminology, a position he retained until 1960. The years in Berkeley produced much of Wilson's important writing. He authored the first two textbooks on police management: the International City Management Association's Municipal Police Administration and Wilson's own book, Police Administration.[12] Police Administration became known nationally as the "bible" of professional policing.[13] Virtually every American police department from the 1950s onward was organized around the principles set forth in Wilson's books.[14]

ESTABLISHING POLICING STANDARDS

In addition to producing the two most influential figures in American policing and the resultant professionalism, California contributed substantially to the articulation of national standards for policing. As previously mentioned, August Vollmer contributed significantly to the body of recommendations for police reform promulgated by the Wickersham Commission. In 1959 California pioneered state-wide legislation that statutorily established minimum standards for entry-level police training by creating the nation's first state Commission on Peace Officer Standards and Training (POST).[15] The creation of POST resulted from efforts of the Peace Officers Association of California (CPOA) which, in 1945, began in earnest to establish policing standards and qualifications. In 1952 CPOA joined forces with the Peace Officers' Research Association of California (PORAC), and the two groups worked diligently in fashioning what evolved as POST.[16] Today, all states have commissions regulating entry-level training.[17] It is interesting to note, also, that the "Law Enforcement Code of Ethics" was a product of a collaborative effort between PORAC and The School of Criminology within the University of California at Berkeley. The Law Enforcement Code of Ethics, formulated in 1956, has been adopted nationally as the standard for ethical conduct.[18]

In 1973 the National Advisory Commission on Criminal Justice Standards and Goals developed national standards to effect improvement in the delivery of police services. Through completion of its report, entitled Police, the commission created a document which any police administrator could access to examine state-of-the-art operational practices. Police filled a void similar to that which had existed 40 years earlier and had been filled by the reports issued by the Wickersham Commission. Interestingly, the Chairman of the Task Force on Police, which researched and prepared Police, was Edward Davis, who at the time was Chief of Police of Los Angeles. Additionally, Chief Davis' staff was largely comprised of persons employed in law enforcement in California.[19]

CRITICAL EVENTS IN THE DEVELOPMENT OF CALIFORNIA POLICE

1847 The state's first police force was formed in San Francisco
1869 The Los Angeles Police Department was created
1910 The nation's first female police officer was appointed to LAPD
1914 August Vollmer begins the nation's first auto patrol in Berkeley
1930 First two-year C.J. college degree at Santa Rosa Junior College
1930 Wickersham Commission issues report on police professionalism
1935 San Jose State offered first bachelors in law enforcement
1950 O.W. Wilson pioneered the field of Police Administration
1959 P.O.S.T. was created

1.2

THE STRUCTURE OF CALIFORNIA'S POLICE

California has been unique in its approach to the configuration of its police function. It has fashioned a system somewhat comparable to the British. Responsibility for police operations remains with the primary police agencies; however, the state has become involved in the administration of the police function in a number of ways: (1) by providing a legal basis for coordinating local agencies through the office of the Attorney General (refined by Attorney General Earl Warren in 1940),[20] (2) by providing criminal information, laboratory and investigation services through the Department of Justice (headed by the Attorney General) and (3) by providing programs for upgrading personnel, programs which are administered chiefly by the Commission on Peace Officer Standards and Training.[21]

DELEGATION OF POLICING RESPONSIBILITIES

While the state has the primary responsibility for maintaining law and order, it has delegated the performance of these responsibilities to the counties and municipalities. The sheriff is the principal constitutional law enforcement officer in each county. As such, he or she has the duty of enforcing all criminal laws within the county, in addition to performing other custodial and civil functions. While the sheriff has county-wide jurisdiction, the policing function is normally performed in unincorporated areas, except when the county contracts with a municipality to provide police services.[22]

STATE-LOCAL AGENCY PARTNERSHIP

California is rather unique also in that a strong partnership between the state and local police agencies has evolved for controlling major criminal activity and improving the performance of other aspects of the police function at the local level. An interdependence and cohesiveness of purpose has developed. Spheres of responsibility have emerged for the state, county and municipal agencies, as well as other special purpose agencies, e.g., transit authorities.[23]

The Department of Justice provides extensive support services to the vast array of local law enforcement agencies throughout the state. These include state-of-the-art crime laboratory services, a central repository of criminal history information and crime statistics, specialized training programs, and intelligence updates.[24]

For purposes of structural analysis, law enforcement agencies within California may be divided into eight categories. The majority (345) of the state's 572 law enforcement agencies may be categorized as municipal police and public safety departments. County sheriff departments total 58. Forty-nine agencies provide policing services on the state's higher education campuses. There are 14 marshal offices throughout the state. Forty-six counties have their own law enforcement investigative operations. There are 27 California state agencies and 33 additional agencies that perform a variety of other specialized services.[25]

NUMBER OF POLICE AGENCIES IN CALIFORNIA & OTHER SELECTED STATES

	Local Agencies	Sheriff	Special Police
Pennsylvania	1,049	66	51
Illinois	748	102	43
Texas	632	255	824
New York	463	57	57
California	345	58	93

Source: U.S. Department of Justice (1992)

According to the 1993 Uniform Crime Reports, California employs an estimated 58,769 full-time peace officers. This represents the largest contingent of any state. Additionally, according to the same source, an estimated 26,981 civilians are employed in support of law enforcement operations. Again, this number leads the nation.[26] It should be noted that these estimated figures are less by several thousands than those figures compiled by the California Commission on Peace Officer Standards and Training, but they are useful for proportionate national comparisons.[27] Nevertheless, it is indisputable that the state of California leads the nation in law enforcement employment figures (as well as population), and this adds to the challenge of a coordinated delivery of services.

THE ARRAY OF AGENCIES

For purposes of general familiarity, California's law enforcement agencies can be divided into the following categories: state, county, municipal, and special district police.

State Agencies

Foremost among state agencies is the Department of Justice. The Division of Law Enforcement, within the Department of Justice, is directly overseen by the state's chief law officer, the Attorney General. The Division of Law Enforcement provides a wide range of support services to local and state enforcement agencies. Primary services consist of investigative services, including offender profiling; narcotic enforcement, which in 1991 resulted in the nation's largest ever methaqualone lab seizure; forensic services, including a state-of-the-art DNA lab; criminal identification, featuring one of the world's most sophisticated automated latent print systems; and criminal information and the Western States Information Network, established by Congress in 1981 as one of the six regional intelligence sharing systems in the United States.[28]

Until July 10, 1995, the California State Police was primarily responsible for protection of state properties and the persons therein. Effective July 10, the California Highway Patrol subsumed the State Police and their responsibilities. Thus in addition to these added responsibilities, the California Highway Patrol has primary responsibility for providing traffic supervision and control on all state highways constructed as freeways and on highways within the unincorporated areas of the state.[29] There are additional state agencies whose employees provide law enforcement services in support of various state endeavors, e.g., Department of Alcoholic Beverage Control, Department of Fish and Game, and the State Lottery.

County Agencies

Just as the Attorney General is the chief law enforcement officer of the state, the sheriff is the chief law enforcement officer within his or her county. Sheriffs are elected public officials whose deputies are responsible for law enforcement throughout the counties in which they function. Sheriffs departments are generally responsible for serving court papers and maintaining security within courtrooms and, of course, also provide patrol services in unincorporated areas of counties. Sheriffs also run county jails and are responsible for more detainees awaiting trial than any other type of law enforcement department in the country. The Los Angeles County jail system is the largest in the world, and from 1987 has had daily average populations exceeding 20,000 inmates.[30]

Other county agencies include district attorney investigators, coroner staff, and fraud investigators. In addition, marshal departments are found in 14 counties. Marshals are empowered to enforce the orders of the courts of the state in the more populous counties.[31]

Municipal Agencies

There are 345 municipal police departments in California. Six agencies employ more than 1,000 peace officers per agency, while 106 agencies employ fewer than 25 sworn personnel. The remaining 233 police agencies employ between 25 and 999 officers. Thus, there is tremendous diversity among agencies in terms of personnel, equipment, and services.

Viewing California's municipal agencies in a national perspective reveals some most interesting facts. Three of the 15 largest municipal police departments are in California (Los Angeles, San Francisco, and San Diego). Even more interesting is the ratio of sworn personnel to the population served. In this regard, the city of San Diego ranks number one with the lowest ratio, i.e., 1.5 sworn officers per 1,000 citizens. Los Angeles is third in this category with a ratio of 2.1 officers per 1,000 citizens (San Francisco is not far behind with a 2.4 ratio). In comparison, the ratios of New York and Chicago Police Departments (the nation's two largest agencies) are 3.8 and 4.1 per 1,000 citizens, respectively.[32] Certainly, California's large agencies are performing the policing task with a high degree of efficiency, comparatively. Municipal police have the heaviest responsibility for dealing with crime and the greatest order maintenance responsibilities. Municipal police are also the most important element of policing in terms of public image and political significance.[33]

CALIFORNIA'S LARGEST POLICE DEPARTMENTS

Agency:	Full-Time Sworn Officers
Los Angeles Police Department	8,295
Los Angeles Sheriffs Department	7,440
California Highway Patrol	5,958
San Diego Police Department	1,816
San Francisco Police Department	1,777
San Jose Police Department	1,110

Source: Sourcebook of Criminal Justice Statistics (1993)

Special District Police

Special district police forces are often located in the same area as city police or county sheriff departments, but they have separate responsibilities.[34] Within California, the most common forms of special district police are transit police, housing authorities, park police, public school security and campus police. In some instances, these forces can be quite large. For example, the Los Angeles Airport Police Department consists of 237 peace officers, and the Los Angeles County Metropolitan Transit Authority consists of 276 peace officers and continues to expand. The Los Angeles Unified School District Police Department tops both the foregoing with a complement of 294 sworn employees.[35]

"PRIVATE" POLICING IN CALIFORNIA

Private police constitute a crucial form of enforcement activity in California. The role of private protection is extensive and consists of three elements: security, safety and emergency planning. Security includes physical plant security, crime prevention, executive protection and internal investigations. Safety aspects include accident prevention, hazardous materials recognition and compliance with OSHA regulations and general industry safety orders. Emergency planning entails readiness for unusual incidents and emergency response to unusual incidents.[36]

Private security is a rapidly expanding business in California. Two of the top five security companies in the United States are Pinkerton's and American Protective Services, headquartered in California. Pinkerton, which attained number one status in a recently conducted survey of revenues, exemplifies a full service California-based private security company. As a result of its full range and quality of services, Pinkerton has become an industry leader with more than 20,000 customers around the world and counts half the "Fortune 500" companies as its clients. To meet its customer demand, Pinkerton employs 45,000 security and investigative personnel from 220 offices worldwide. A little known and most interesting side-bar to the Pinkerton success story is that Pinkerton has really been a subsidiary of California Plant Protection (CPP) since 1986 when CPP purchased Pinkerton. The name "Pinkerton" was retained because of its reputation and name recognition value.[37]

A common deficiency throughout the nation in the area of private policing is the lack of personnel standards. Requirements for employment are minimal and in many cases, training is nonexistent.[38] California is among the states beginning to establish standards. The Public Training Officers Association of San Diego has developed an excellent five-week, 180-hour training course. A number of contract protection firms and corporations send their officers through this training program.[39]

Pinkerton Security and Investigation Services has developed sophisticated employee selection processes to measure candidates' attitudes toward job stability, integrity, policy compliance, work ethics, and career ambition. Pinkerton has also developed exceptional field officer and management training courses.[40]

Private security is now undergoing many of the changes which have already occurred within public law enforcement operations. Heightened entry requirements, mandated training, and legislative regulation are all leading to increased professionalism. Municipal departments have undertaken concerted efforts to involve private security organizations in their crime detection and prevention efforts, and indications are that private security will soon assume a legitimate place alongside other police agencies in the eyes of the public.[41]

1.3

CALIFORNIA POLICE ADMINISTRATION

HISTORICAL ADMINISTRATIVE ERAS

In his textbook entitled Criminal Justice Today, Frank Schmalleger began discussion of the theme of police administration in the context of a recently convened symposium on American policing at Harvard University's Kennedy School of Government.[42] This is an ideal starting point for discussion of this complex theme and one that is also ideal for discussing policing in California since the eras' time parameters were significantly influenced by events occurring in California, e.g., August Vollmer's rallying of police executives around the idea of reform during the 1920s and early 1930s. Reports derived from the symposium entitled Perspectives in Policing divided policing into three eras.

The Political Era

The first policing era, the "political era," was characterized by close ties between police and public officials. It began in the 1840s and ended approximately 1930. Throughout the period police departments generally served the interests of powerful politicians, while providing order maintenance services almost as an afterthought.[43] Illustrative of this era was the notorious "machine" that operated in Los Angeles during the decades of the early 20th Century. The machine was comprised of individuals who maintained open vice conditions in the center of the Los Angeles business district through the successive administrations of six mayors. Those who exercised control were referred to as the "bosses." The bosses granted protection, issued orders to high city officials, arranged appointments to office, and made promotions. An editorial in the "Hollywood Citizen-News" captures the essence of this milieu:

> "When a mayor accepts campaign funds from the gamblers and prostitutes and in return appoints members of a police commission who are approved by the vice leaders, and the police commissioners in turn appoint a chief of police approved by the vice leaders, and the chief of police in turn appoints members of the vice squad approved by the vice leaders, a situation exists which makes it impossible for the mayor, members of the police commission, the chief of police, and members of the vice squad to face charges of open vice without attempts to falsify."[44]

The influence of each historical phase identified by the Harvard team survives today in what James Q. Wilson calls styles of policing. Wilson cited the "watchman" style" as characteristic of the political era.[45] This style makes considerable use of "informal" police intervention, including persuasion and threats. Critics contend that this style is unfairly found today in lower class communities, especially where interpersonal relations may include a fair amount of violence. Others, however, have pointed out that in responding to the mandate for order maintenance, the police create a sense of community that makes social life possible.[46]

THE REFORM ERA

The second period, the "reform era," began in the 1930s and lasted until the 1970s. The reform era was characterized by pride in professional crime fighting. Using the focus on criminal law as a basic source of police legitimacy, police in the reform era moved to narrow their functioning to crime control and criminal apprehension. Activities that drew the police into solving other kinds of community problems and relied on other kinds of responses were identified as "social work," and became the object of derision. During the era of reform policing, the new model demanded an impartial law enforcer who related to citizens in professionally neutral and distant terms. No better characterization of this model can be found than television's "Sergeant Friday," whose response, "Just the facts, ma"am," typified an ideal impersonal and crime-solving posture.[47]

Again Los Angeles' experiences provide insights into the impact of the reform era on police administration. In 1923 August Vollmer was appointed Chief of Police of Los Angeles for a one-year term to effect needed reforms. This appointment provided a major metropolitan testing ground for his newly developed theories of police administration. Vollmer reorganized the Los Angeles Police Department to include two key ingredients: efficient administration and scientific administration. He developed new concepts utilizing existing resources. Using statistics compiled by his newly appointed statistician, a 300-person mobile "Crime Crushers" division was formed. Armed with the knowledge of when and where crimes were most frequently committed, these "crime-crushing" officers saturated target areas. Criminals were arrested, property recovered, and crime in targeted areas was substantially reduced.

Vollmer organized the police department into 11 divisions, each uniting similar functions under a single head. To select the right applicants to implement these tasks, Vollmer called for individual exams by trained psychologists to eliminate the unqualified. After one year of service, Vollmer, true to his word, resigned as Chief of Police and returned to Berkeley. His basic theories of scientific methods of detection, administration, and selection/training of officers had been accepted and had been proved workable within a large metropolitan agency.[48]

The Los Angeles Police Department eventually evolved to become the epitome of reform era policing under the direction of William H. Parker. When Parker became chief in 1950, he declared that he would make the Los Angeles Police Department the most respected police force in the United States. In 1960, he was the only representative of municipal law enforcement in the United States invited to participate in the 29th General Assembly of the International Police Organization (Interpol) in Washington, D.C. In 1964, he was the first United States police administrator chosen to assist the country of India in redeveloping that nation's police procedures. The Indian government selected Parker, lauding him as the only acceptable police administrator in the United States. Parker's death in 1966 ended what was possibly the most productive and renowned period in the history of municipal law enforcement.[49]

The prominence of California in effecting crucial progress during the reform era was highlighted in 1971 when Los Angeles County Sheriff Peter Pitchess was selected by Jerris

Leonard, Administrator of the Law Enforcement Assistance Administration, to serve as a vice chairman of the National Advisory Commission on Criminal Justice Standards and Goals (under the chairmanship of Russel Peterson, Governor of Delaware). The Commission was created to formulate for the first time national criminal justice standards and goals for crime reduction and prevention at the state and local levels. Selected as chairman of the task force on police was Los Angeles chief of police Edward Davis. The vast majority of Davis' nationally represented task force staff was comprised of police practitioners from California. The final product of the task force, published in 1973 as the Report on Police, promulgated national standards that represented the most up-to-date and proven experience in the police field.[50]

In terms of Wilson's policing styles, the "legalistic" style would be descriptive of the reform era. This style is marked by a strict concern with enforcing the precise "letter of the law." Legalistic departments, however, may assume a "hands-off" approach to otherwise disruptive or problematic forms of behavior that are not violations of the criminal law.[51]

THE COMMUNITY-PROBLEM SOLVING ERA

The final era--one which is just beginning--is the "community problem-solving" era. The community problem-solving approach to police work stresses the service role of police officers and envisions a partnership between police and the community. It is based on the premise that both the police and the community must work together to identify, prioritize, and solve contemporary problems such as crime, drugs, fear of crime, social and physical disorder, and overall neighborhood decay, with the goal of improving the overall quality of life in the area.[52]

Research conducted during the 1970s suggested that one factor could help police improve their record in dealing with crime: information. If information about crime and criminals could be obtained from citizens by police and could be properly managed by police departments, investigative and other units could significantly increase their effect on crime. Moreover, research into foot patrol suggested that at least part of the fear reduction potential was linked to the order maintenance activities of foot patrol officers. The findings of fear reduction and foot patrol experiments, when coupled with the research on the relationship between fear and disorder (gangs, prostitutes, etc.), provided opportunities for police to understand the increasing concerns of citizens' groups about disorder.[53] Largely through the coordinative efforts of Professor Robert Trojanowicz, Michigan State University, community policing evolved to its current status as rapidly becoming the predominant operating philosophy of police agencies.[54]

In the aftermath of the 1991 Rodney King incident, California Attorney General Daniel Lungren became the first attorney general in the nation to promote the concept of community policing.[55] California cities that have implemented exemplary programs of community policing include San Diego, Santa Barbara, Santa Ana, Garden Grove and Hayward.[56] In the context of Wilson's three classifications of policing styles, the "service" style is most descriptive of the community problem-solving approach. This style of policing is marked by a concern with helping rather than strict enforcement. Service-oriented agencies are more likely to take advantage of community resources than are other types of departments.[57]

1.4

CALIFORNIA'S POLICING INNOVATIONS

California is unique among the states in terms of its quantity of innovative contributions to policing. As previously mentioned, August Vollmer is indisputably considered the father of American policing. His array of contributions, both in terms of human resource development and crime prevention programs/equipment development, remains unparalleled. Clearly, Vollmer set the pace for the professionalization of policing.

HUMAN RESOURCE DEVELOPMENT AND ENHANCEMENT

California's lead role in the creation of standards for policing has been previously highlighted, e.g., POST and leadership in the National Advisory Commission on Criminal Justice Standards and Training. Possibly not as widely known is the extent to which California has contributed to development of programs of officer "survival," of both the tactical and mental health varieties.

Officer Survival

In 1973 the California Specialized Training Institute introduced the prototype officer survival course in the nation. The course developed was the result of a study of peace officer on-duty deaths in California conducted by the Institute faculty. The 40-hour course drew students not only from California, but from 49 states and 27 foreign countries, as well.[58]

Another significant program to enhance officer safety (as well as citizen protection) was created in 1967 by the Los Angeles Police Department. The program, popularly known as Special Weapons and Tactics (SWAT), was developed in response to the increased incidence of urban violence. The primary functions of SWAT teams include protection of police officers from snipers during crowd control, rescue of hostages, neutralization of guerrilla or terrorist operations, nonviolent apprehension of desperate barricaded suspects, and rescue of officers or citizens endangered by gunfire.[59]

The increased movement of police work toward the helping professions highlighted the importance of interpersonal skills, psychological astuteness, and emotional control. Traditionally, police administrators were reluctant to acknowledge that their employees (and themselves) were suffering from personal problems. In fact, a police chaplain's first attempt at creating a police stress program in New York City in 1958 failed to materialize. In 1968 the Los Angeles Police Department became the first agency to provide free, voluntary psychological counseling services under the direction of Martin Reiser, the nation's first police psychologist. This program became the prototype for other cities.[60]

Cultural Awareness

In California, demographers predict that by the year 2005 there will be no single racial or ethnic group constituting the majority. California law enforcement agencies have recognized the diversity that exists within the state and have developed prototype training programs to enhance officer-citizen interactions and service delivery. The Los Angeles County Sheriff's Department has developed cultural diversity training for recruits and in-service officers. They also developed a 48-hour cultural diversity instructor class certified by the state. The sheriff's department has a Cultural Advisory Committee consisting of 45 persons representing the diversity of Los Angeles. The Committee meets monthly to discuss methods to improve training and review any proposed cultural training materials.

In 1986-1987 16 hours of cultural awareness training were provided to all 200 police personnel of the City of Concord, California. Large components of the course were designed by minority community members on the subjects of which they were to be presenters.[61]

CRIME PREVENTION PROGRAMS AND SPECIALIZED EQUIPMENT

California has been the point of origin for a veritable "who's who" of crime prevention programs and specialized equipment. Renown crime prevention programs include Neighborhood Watch,[62] Mothers Against Drunk Drivers (MADD),[63] and Drug Abuse Resistance Education (DARE).[64]

In terms of equipment innovations, it was previously mentioned that August Vollmer introduced the nation's first automobile patrol service, as well as the first scientific crime laboratory. Another equipment item of exceptional value to cities larger than 10 square miles or with populations exceeding 50,000 persons is the helicopter. Use of the helicopter for police patrol, rather than for traffic surveillance, was perfected in the Los Angeles area by both the Los Angeles Police and Sheriff's Departments. The most striking illustration of the crime deterrent capability of helicopters was provided through Project Sky Knight in the city of Lakewood (a contract city of the Los Angeles County Sheriff's Department). During an 18-month study period beginning in 1966, the crime rate per 100,000 population decreased by 11 percent in Lakewood, while it increased eight percent countywide. Clearly, California has been extraordinarily progressive in its policing practices. Its innovations have benefitted not only the residents of California but it has been the leader in exportation of innovative policing concepts throughout the nation.[65]

EMERGENCY MANAGEMENT

The term "emergency management" refers to the process of governmental control of disasters. Local, state, and federal governments combine to manage disasters through orchestrated processes of mitigation, preparedness, response, and recovery.[66] In a sense, the term "emergency" is really a misnomer in that disastrous incidents normally far exceed the control capabilities of any single governmental agency normally involved in the delivery of emergency services, e.g., local law enforcement or local fire services. Nevertheless, within the special context of emergency management, "emergency" actually connotes a disastrous incident that exceeds the capabilities of a single agency to handle.

California is a state that has become synonymous with disastrous events. Indeed, it would not be altogether surprising if a grass roots initiative were launched to change the state's name from "California" to "Emergency," i.e., the state of "Emergency." Facetious as the foregoing statement may be, California's law enforcement agencies assume a lead role in the multi-agency response to disasters, particularly civil disorders, earthquakes, terrorism, and on-highway hazardous material spills.[67] Service as a peace officer within California virtually assures immersion in catastrophic emergencies.

One does not need to search deeper than the decade of the 1990s to find examples of sustained widespread dedication of California's law enforcement resources to contend with catastrophic incidents. As an example, during 1992 Los Angeles was the site of a massive civil disturbance that proved to be the costliest civil unrest in U.S. history in terms of personal and property losses. In fact, the 775 million in insurance claims submitted made the civil disorder the fifth most costly catastrophe in U.S. history. Only four natural disasters exceeded the dollar loss.[68]

Less than two years after the massive civil disorder, the most destructive earthquake in the modern history of Los Angeles rumbled across the landscape.[69] In a matter of 10 seconds, Southern California sustained a devastatingly crippling blow. Barely beyond the recovery phase of the civil disturbance, California's law enforcement resources were rededicated to control of yet another catastrophic event.

Pictured above: Damaged Los Angeles freeway overpass produced by the Northridge Earthquake (Photo courtesy of LAPD)

At the time of this writing, the entire state of California was "held hostage" to the terroristic threats of the notorious "Unabomber." In fact, the California-based Unabomber had effectively disrupted air travel and mail services internationally when, on June 27, 1995, he sent a letter to the "San Francisco Chronicle" threatening to blow up an airliner at Los Angeles International Airport. The deployment of law enforcement resources to counter the threat was extensive, particularly since the threat came on the heels of the tragic Oklahoma City bombing.[70]

Civil disturbances and earthquakes are the most potentially disruptive large-scale emergency events with which law enforcement must be prepared to contend. In a recent Delphi exercise conducted at the FBI Academy in Virginia, a panel of law enforcement managers, scholars, and executives constructed a scenario of lawlessness for the year 2000 that will feature frequent urban unrest and civil disorder episodes throughout California and the United States.[71] Regarding earthquakes, despite the killer earthquakes that have steadily occurred throughout California in recent decades, the "big one" that is overdue to strike looms as the largest disaster in American history. When it occurs (and it is a virtual certainty to occur) the entire nation will suffer a serious setback.[72]

Pictured above: LAPD officers in riot formation protecting headquarters (Parker Center). (Photo courtesy of LAPD)

Law enforcement, in general, is experiencing markedly fewer emergency events which the assets of a single police department or sheriff's office can control. Advancing technology has virtually forced the issue of multi-agency, multi-jurisdictional emergency management upon law enforcement, along with other agencies/departments with emergency management responsibilities.

The mechanism for marshalling law enforcement agencies from outside an impacted area is referred to as a mutual aid agreement. Mutual aid pacts are activated when a chief of police or sheriff determines that an emergency situation within his or her jurisdiction may become or is already beyond the control of agency resources. Additional resources are subsequently allocated to the requesting agency through a hierarchical governmental network coordinated by the Law Enforcement Branch of the Governor's Office of Emergency Services.[73]

The Standardized Emergency Management System (SEMS) is the multilevel organizational framework for coordinating state and local emergency response operations in California. The purpose of SEMS is to enhance the flow of emergency information and the effective and efficient use of mutual aid resources.[74]

Law enforcement responsibilities in the context of emergency management typically include evacuations, perimeter and traffic control, security, and investigation and apprehension of law violators.[75] The details of emergency response should be worked out through the development of the department's emergency plan and training exercises so that roles and actions will not have to be clarified in the midst of an emergency response. A department's level of readiness to respond is directly related to the effectiveness of its training program.[76]

Pictured above: LAPD motorcycle officers patrol South Central L.A. in the aftermath of the riot. (Photo courtesy of LAPD)

1.5

CRITICAL AND LEGAL ISSUES IN CALIFORNIA POLICING

CRITICAL ISSUES FOR THE FUTURE

In 1994 the California Peace Officers Association (CPOA) completed an advisory strategic plan for California policing through the 1990s. The plan was constructed to provide government agencies, voters, and the taxpaying public a direction for positive change in the 1990s and beyond. The plan is impressive because of its scope of coverage and its three main topical areas: "Changing the Police Organization, "Keeping the Peace," and "Understanding Society." This categorization represents formal acknowledgement by the leading association of California peace officers of the expanded role of the police that lies at the core of community-oriented policing. Review of the recommendations yields significant insights into the critical issues that must be addressed today by California law enforcement.[77]

Fifteen recommendations comprised the strategic plan's first section, "Changing the Police Organization." At the heart of these recommendations were issues relative to enhancing employee performance and health. The threshold issue was management's recognition that employees are an organization's most valuable asset. In this context, agency-specific recruitment and training programs were called for, as well as objective-based performance evaluations and procedures for rewarding high achievers and for accomplishing remediation when warranted. In the same vein, disciplinary systems must ensure fairness, and training should be used extensively to correct transgressions.

Employee health emerged as an important issue. Fairness in shift assignments was urged, and permanent shift assignments of six months or longer were preferred to allow for stability in the social lives and biorhythms of officers. Two recommendations specifically focused on stress reduction, to be accomplished by more mutually developed (management and line officers) internal operating procedures and increased development of counseling and employee assistance programs.

The second part of the strategic plan addressed the concept of "keeping the peace." At the heart of this portion of the plan was adoption of community policing by all California law enforcement agencies. Within this recommendation, however, the fact that community policing is labor-intensive was fully noted, as well as the related difficulty in its implementation in larger agencies.[78] Certainly, budget constraints, work load demands, personnel shortages and turnover, and questionable support from line officers are but a few formidable barriers to implementation. In fact, in recognition of these obstacles, some have envisioned creation of teams of sworn problem-solving specialists to perform problem-solving aspects of community policing while other officers serve as emergency response specialists. Job rotation would be a means for involving all officers in both assignments.[79] Nevertheless, CPOA has committed fully to the core elements of community policing and embraces it as the emergent policing style statewide.

Altogether, seven recommendations comprised the "Keeping the Peace" section of the strategic plan. It is most interesting and insightful that three of the seven focused on emergency management issues. One called for continued training and planning for natural and man-made disasters. Another recommendation strongly endorsed sole use of the Incident Command System for command and control of multi-agency responders and strongly encouraged strengthening of mutual aid agreements. A third recommendation envisioned civil disorder as a looming trend in social behavior and accordingly called for extensive training and practice in humane crowd and riot control techniques. Rounding out the recommendations in this category was expansion of crime prevention programs such as DARE.

The third portion of the strategic plan examined methods for better understanding society. At the center of these eight recommendations were methods for enhancing officers' cultural sensitivities. Similarly, methods were suggested for assuring the needs of the community were being met. Both juveniles and the elderly were identified as special populations that warranted special focused attention. Also, within this category of enhancing services to the community through improved understanding of society, community-based measures for increasing revenues for law enforcement operations were examined.[80]

From review of CPOA's recommendations for California law enforcement, it may be observed that the following constitute key focal areas for present and future law enforcement operations in California: human resource development and nurturing, supportive management practices, community policing, emergency management, cultural/community sensitivity, and efficient use of policing resources.

LEGAL ISSUES

The legal environment surrounding the police acts to help ensure proper official conduct. Inappropriate behavior on the part of police officers can later become the basis for civil or criminal action against the employing agency and the concerned officer.

The beating of Rodney King by several Los Angeles police officers has proved to be a landmark in the recent history of law enforcement and the quintessential example of the legal milieu within which an officer's actions are assessed. In fact, many observers believe that some day the history of policing will be delineated in "pre-Rodney King" and "post-Rodney King" terms.[81]

There are unique aspects of police work, elements of an officer's job that no other societal body is allowed to perform: the use of deadly force and the capability to engage in high-speed pursuits. These unique policing activities, the consequences of which can prove deadly to citizens if improperly exercised, routinely expose police officers to extreme civil and criminal liability if not executed within established guidelines. The following discussion will examine these crucial areas of liability.

Use of Force

In a complex urban society, officers are confronted daily with situations where control must be exercised to effect arrests and to protect the public safety. Control may be achieved through advice, warnings, and persuasion, or by the use of physical force. According to California Penal Code Section 835a, officers may use physical force to effect an arrest, prevent escape, or overcome resistance.[82]

Two key elements of use of force policies are (1) the reasonableness and necessity of force used and (2) the level of force used. While the use of reasonable physical force may be necessary in situations which cannot otherwise be controlled, force may not be resorted to unless other reasonable alternatives have been exhausted or would clearly be ineffective under the particular circumstances. Additionally, an officer is required to react to a suspect's behavior with the minimum amount of force necessary to control the suspect.[83]

Pictured above: Officers make a "mass arrest" of alleged California gang members.
(Photo courtesy of LAPD)

Use of Force Options

The array of use of force options available to an officer can be categorized into five levels: (1) verbalization; (2) firm grip; (3) compliance techniques, including wristlocks, twistlocks, and chemical agents; (4) intermediate force, including batons, kicks, tasers, saps, leg sweeps and swarm techniques; and (5) deadly force, including firearms and upper body control holds. The selection of an option must be made in consideration of using only the minimal level of force required to gain compliance with the concerned officers' instructions. As a suspect escalates or de-escalates his or her level of resistance or aggressiveness, the officers must react accordingly.[84]

Deadly Force

In California a peace officer is authorized to use deadly force when it reasonably appears necessary to protect the officer or others from an immediate threat of death or serious bodily injury; to prevent a crime where the suspect's actions place persons in jeopardy of death or serious bodily injury; to apprehend a fleeing felon for a crime involving serious bodily injury or where there is a substantial risk that the person whose arrest is sought will cause death or serious bodily injury to others if apprehension is delayed.[85]

The fleeing felon rule has historically applied to most U.S. jurisdictions. It held that officers could use deadly force to prevent the escape of a suspected felon, even when the person represented no immediate threat to the officer or to the public. The fleeing felon rule stemmed from early common law punishments which specified death for a large number of crimes. Modernly, the fleeing felon rule has been called into question in a number of courts. The 1985 Supreme Court case of Tennessee v. Garner specified the conditions under which deadly force could be used in the apprehension of suspected felons. The Court held that the use of deadly force by the police to prevent the escape of a fleeing felon might be justified only where the suspect could reasonably be thought to represent a significant threat of serious injury or death to the public or to the officer.[86]

The events surrounding the use of deadly force by police officers have accounted for some of the most expensive damages awarded to plaintiffs, and training has emerged as critically important not only in defending against lawsuits, but also in providing professional police service to the community. The technology and various means exist for ensuring that both new and veteran police officers receive adequate training. Although not all agencies have the luxury of high-tech training, abundant in-house training, or an in-house legal advisor, agency administrators are nonetheless responsible for obtaining adequate training for their personnel. Clearly, training must be assigned a priority of the highest level.[87]

Pursuits

Until the 1980s very little was known about the risks and benefits of pursuit driving. The current legal trend, i.e., balancing the enforcement of laws with the safety of the public, has resulted in a number of restrictions being placed on pursuits. In fact, the more that is learned about vehicular pursuits, the more controls are placed on them. The analogy of a pursuit to the use of a firearm has demonstrated their potential deadly consequences.

During 1994, according to the California Highway Patrol, there were 8,079 pursuits statewide. In the course of these pursuits, 132 officers were injured, 27 suspects were killed, and 765 other suspects were injured. In addition, 421 uninvolved motorists and pedestrians were caught in the path of police pursuits; twelve of these persons suffered fatal injuries.[88] These figures speak for themselves in pointing to the inherent dangerousness of pursuits.

Section 21055 of the California Vehicle Code (V.C.) specifies that in emergency situations the driver of an authorized emergency vehicle is exempt from the "rules of the road," provided that the red light and siren of the vehicle are activated. Section 21056 V.C., however, specifies that this exemption does not relieve the driver from the duty to drive with due regard for the safety of all persons using the highway, nor does it protect him or her from the privileges granted in Section 21055 V.C.[89]

Pursuits should be initiated only when law violators clearly exhibit an intention to avoid arrest by using a vehicle to flee, or when suspected law violators refuse to stop and use a vehicle to flee. Officers must weigh the seriousness of the offense against the potential dangers to themselves or innocent citizens if they elect to pursue.[90] The policy issue confronting law enforcement and municipal administrators is a familiar one of balancing conflicting interests. On one side there is the need to apprehend known offenders. On the other side, there is the safety of innocent bystanders, law enforcement officers, and fleeing drivers and their passengers. While they to date have maintained a "middle-of-the-road posture," law enforcement administrators must be prepared to make difficult decisions based on the costs and benefits of these types of pursuit to the public they serve.[91]

Other Sources of Liability

In addition to use of force and vehicular pursuits, liability frequently arises from discriminatory practices relative to recruitment, selection, retention, and promotion of police personnel. In addition, sexual harassment and discriminatory practices involving the disabled are rapidly emerging areas of litigation.[92] While these areas do not routinely offer the potential for physical harm, they, nonetheless, can result in the imposition of severe sanctions for transgressions. Certainly, too, the trauma suffered by victims can last as long as the effects of physical injuries. As is the case with the use of force and pursuits, the best way to prevent liability from arising due to discriminatory personnel practices is to establish and disseminate clear written policies on the relevant topics. The written guidance must then be followed up with appropriate training sessions. Failure to address areas of potential liability can result in losses far in excess of publication and training costs.

2.1

THE STRUCTURE OF CALIFORNIA'S COURTS

COURT STRUCTURE

Like their counterparts in all of the Federal and most other state systems, California courts are organized into a three-tiered structure consisting of (1) trial courts, (2) intermediate courts of appeal and (3) a state supreme court. Each of these levels has its own jurisdiction, or power to hear and rule on a case. California's trial courts have "original jurisdiction." This means that trial courts possess the authority to preside over cases when they first enter the system. The two courts above the trial courts (i.e., Appellate and Supreme Court) have virtually all of the State's "appellate jurisdiction." In other words, these courts have the power to review the decisions made by the trial courts.[93]

THE FIRST TIER: TRIAL COURTS

Inferior Courts: Justice and Municipal

The trial courts are divided into two levels: inferior courts and superior courts. Inferior courts consist of justice and municipal courts. The justice and municipal courts have only limited jurisdiction. Judges presiding over these courts are restricted to trying only adult criminal cases up to the misdemeanor level. However, justice and municipal courts may preside over the preliminary matters of felony cases. For example, felony suspects are first brought before (i.e., arraigned) municipal court judges before being "held to answer" in Superior Court. Also, the preliminary hearings of such high-profile cases as The McMartin Pre-School case and the O.J. Simpson double-murder case were first adjudicated in municipal court.

The only difference between the justice and municipal courts is the population of the regions they serve. Justice courts are located in districts of 40,000 or less. Municipal courts preside over districts populated by 40,000 or more. To become either a Justice or Municipal Court Judge, one must have been a member of the California Bar or bench for at least five years. These judges are subject to the vote at every general election.[94]

Superior Courts

Above the justice and municipal courts are California's superior courts. These tribunals have more limited jurisdiction than do superior courts in many other states. Instead of having the authority to hear all criminal cases, California superior court judges are restricted to trying felony cases. Superior courts hear misdemeanor matters in only limited circumstances. However, superior court judges preside over misdemeanor appeals. To become a Superior Court Judge, one must have previously been a member of the bar or bench for 10 years. These judges are up for election every six years.[95]

THE SECOND TIER: COURTS OF APPEAL

The middle tier in the California court system is inhabited by the Court of Appeal. As its name indicates, this court possesses "appellate jurisdiction." Unlike the trial courts, which are run by a single judge, California's appellate courts are known as "collegial bodies." That is, court outcomes are decided by a panel of judges (rather than a single judge).

A panel of three judges is used to decide cases before the Court of Appeals. These judges, because of their higher stature in the system, are referred to by the title of "Justice." Each three member panel consists of a Presiding Justice and two Associate Justices. Agreement by a majority (2 out of 3) is needed to render a judgement. Justices of the Court of Appeal are elected every 12 years.[96]

THE THIRD TIER: THE CALIFORNIA SUPREME COURT

The highest level in the California court system is reserved for the Supreme Court. This court has the ultimate power to review over issues of state subject matter. It reviews cases it chooses to hear from the California appellate courts. Furthermore, it has automatic and direct appellate jurisdiction of death penalty cases. The Supreme Court has seven members, one Chief Justice and six Associate Justices. Concurrence of four justices is necessary for a judgement.

Justices of the Supreme Court are elected by popular vote every 12 years. Although re-election is generally much more assured than in the other branches of government, it is by no means automatic. An example of the significant impact of these elections occurred when Chief Justice Rose Byrd and several of her associate justices were not re-elected.[97]

ANNUAL PAY FOR JUDGES IN CALIFORNIA AND SELECTED STATES (1994)

	Supreme Court	Appellate Court	Trial Court
California	$127,267	$119,314	$104,262
New York	$120,000	$110,750	$104,000
Michigan	$111,941	$107,463	$ 98,844
Alabama	$107,125	$106,125	$ 72,500
Alaska	$104,472	$ 98,688	$ 96,600

Source: National Center for State Courts (1994)

CALIFORNIA COURT STRUCTURE, 1993

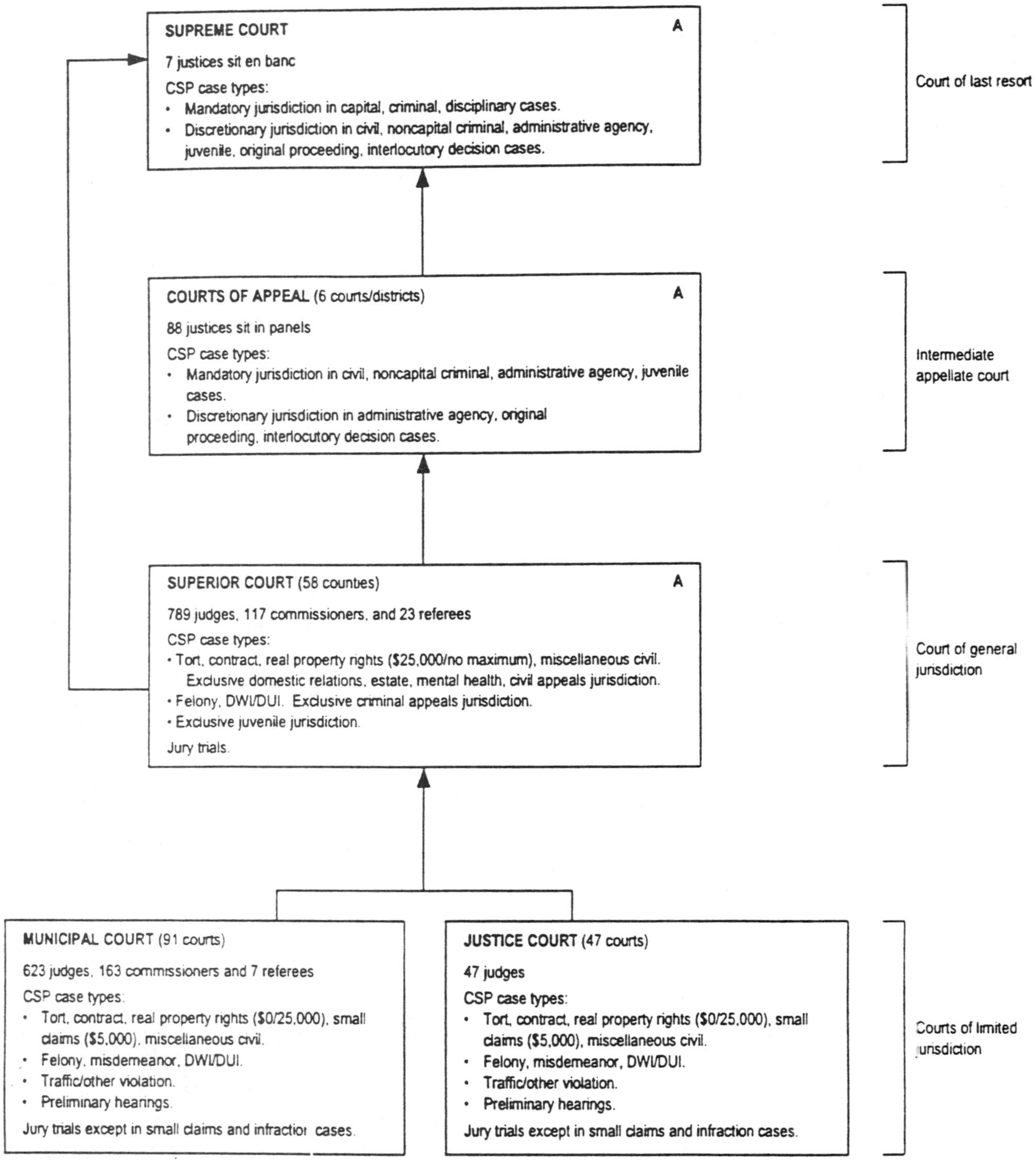

Source: National Center For State Courts (1995)

2.2

PRETRIAL ACTIVITIES: CUSTODY, BOOKING AND BAIL

THE ARREST WARRANT AND BOOKING

Once a crime is brought to law enforcement's attention, a suspect is often arrested. Both under the California and United States Constitutions, a person may be legally arrested with or without an arrest warrant. If a person is arrested without a warrant, which is the usual case, prior judicial determination of probable cause has not occurred. The United States Supreme Court, in a case originating in California called Riverside v. McLaughlin,[98] decided that people in custody who are arrested without a warrant deserved "prompt" judicial determination of probable cause for their arrest. This means that in-custody arrestees have a right, generally within 48 hours of arrest, to have a judge review police documents to ensure probable cause supported their arrest. Such a procedure is now called a "probable cause determination."

Once suspects are arrested, they are transported to jail or a detention facility. Small police departments typically transport suspects directly to county jail. Medium and large police agencies usually maintain their own jails or "lock-ups" where suspects are held for a short period of time (usually not more than one week) before they are transported to county jail. Next, the suspect is "booked." In California, like in most other states, booking involves photographing and fingerprinting the suspect as well as making an official record of the suspect's charges. The suspect's fingerprints are also run through the Cal Id System (the state-wide computerized fingerprint identification system). This is done to determine if the suspect's fingerprints match those taken from crime scenes throughout the State. In small police agencies and county jails, the booking of a suspect usually takes no more than an hour. However, due to the tremendous backlog of suspects in the Los Angeles area, booking time at the Los Angeles County Jail is usually no less than eight hours and can be more than one full day on busy holidays and weekends.

BAIL AND PRETRIAL RELEASE

Once crime suspects have been arrested and their booking completed, the decision is made whether or not to grant the suspect pretrial release. Although the Eighth Amendment and California Constitution prohibit "excessive bail," numerous court decisions have upheld the right to deny the release of certain classes of suspects before trial. In California, these suspects are:

- o Persons who if released from custody may be a danger either to themselves, to victims/witnesses or to the community;
- o Persons who have been released from custody on prior occasions and have failed to make their required court appearances;
- o Persons charged with first-degree murder.[99]

Suspects who do not fall into the above categories will generally be granted some form of pretrial release. The following are among the most common methods used in California:

1. CASH BAIL: Suspects are required to give a specific amount of money (bail) to authorities in order to secure their release and to guarantee that they will make all of their required court appearances. The specific amount of money, or bail, required for release is written in a document called a "bail schedule." Typically, more serious offenses require more bail than less serious offenses. However, the amount of bail for a given offense will vary from county to county. This is because the "bail schedules" are set at the county level. For example, a person charged with spousal abuse in Los Angeles County must post a $50,000 bail. On the other hand, the same offense committed only minutes away in Orange County requires a $10,000 bail.

Bail can be given either in the form of a full cash payment to the court or in the form of a "bail bond" obtained from a "bail bondsman." California bail bondsmen are licensed by the California Department of Insurance. They charge a fee of 10% of the full bail amount to post a "bail bond" with the court to secure the suspect's release. The 10% fee is not refundable to the suspect, and is considered a "charge." If the suspect fails to appear to required court hearings, the bail bondsman must pay the court the full amount of the bail within 185 days. This is why many bondsmen retain the help of a "bounty hunter" in an attempt to locate the fleeing suspect. If the suspect is located and surrendered to the court within 185 days, the bondsman is not required to pay the full bail to the court.[100]

2. OWN RECOGNIZANCE (OR): First-offenders, misdemeanants and low grade felons are usually granted "OR" pretrial release. This means that the court has accepted the suspect's "word" that he or she will appear in court when required to do so. Persons who have prior histories of failures to appear are not typically granted "OR" release.

Pictured above: A typical California bail bond agency, regulated by the Department of Insurance

2.3

ARRAIGNING & FILING CHARGES AGAINST THE SUSPECT

ARRAIGNMENT OF THE SUSPECT

Subjects are arraigned in municipal court within three working days (excluding weekends and holidays) following their arrest. This procedure involves bringing the suspect before a judge at which time the judge notifies the suspect of the crime(s) with which he or she is being charged.

At this time a "case" is formally opened against the suspect. To save time and money, many California courts have started using "video arraignments." These arraignments permit judges to arraign suspects via two-way television while the suspect remains in custody.

FILING CHARGES AGAINST THE SUSPECT

Once a suspect is arrested and processed, the arresting or investigating officer will visit the prosecutor to seek the formal filing of charges. This is a crucial stage in the California criminal justice system because it is here that large numbers of cases are "kicked out" or not filed. Again, it is the prosecutor who is must decide if a particular case is worthy of continuing on in the system.

There are several reasons why California prosecutors may opt to drop a case at the filing stage. First, they are much less likely than the police to have personal involvement in a case. Because prosecutors do not routinely gain first-hand knowledge of victims or offenders, emotions and other extra-legal factors do not generally influence their decision to file.[101]

Second, the primary goal of prosecutors lies in their ability to obtain a conviction. In deciding whether or not to file, California prosecutors must look at much more than just the potential guilt of the suspect. They must also consider the resources of the state and specific prosecutorial policies.

Because prosecutors represent the people of the State of California, they must weigh all factors in deciding if filing is in the "people's" best interest. If the prosecutor decides to file, he or she must then decide how to proceed with the case: whether by way of filing a complaint (which will require a preliminary hearing) or by seeking an indictment (which will require the use of the Grand Jury).

Regardless of how serious the crime, the "complaint" filed against a suspect need not be necessarily lengthy or detailed. For example, presented below is the four-page complaint filed by the Los Angeles District Attorney's Office against O.J. Simpson:

MUNICIPAL COURT OF LOS ANGELES JUDICIAL DISTRICT

COUNTY OF LOS ANGELES, STATE OF CALIFORNIA

THE PEOPLE OF THE STATE OF CALIFORNIA, Plaintiff v. 01 ORENTHAL JAMES SIMPSON, aka O.J. SIMPSON Defendant(s)	Case No. BA097211 FELONY COMPLAINT FOR ARREST WARRANT

The undersigned is informed and believes that:

COUNT 1

On or about June 12, 1994, in the County of Los Angeles, the crime of MURDER, in violation of PENAL CODE SECTION 187(a), a Felony, was committed by ORENTHAL JAMES SIMPSON, who did willfully, unlawfully, and with malice aforethought murder NICOLE BROWN-SIMPSON, a human being.

"NOTICE: The above offense is a serious felony within the meaning of Penal Code section 1192.7(c)(1)."

It is further alleged that in the commission and attempted commission of the above offense, the said defendant(s), ORENTHAL JAMES SIMPSON, personally used a deadly and dangerous weapon(s), to wit, knife, said use not being an element of the above offense, within the meaning of Penal Code section 12022(b) and also causing the above offense to be a serious felony within the meaning of Penal Code section 1192.7(c)(23).

Source: LADAO Press Conference on the Arrest of O.J. Simpson (1994)

COUNT 2

On or about June 12, 1994, in the County of Los Angeles, the crime of MURDER, in violation of PENAL CODE SECTION 187(a), a Felony, was committed by ORENTHAL JAMES SIMPSON, who did willfully, unlawfully, and with malice aforethought murder RONALD LYLE GOLDMAN, a human being.

"NOTICE: The above offense is a serious felony within the meaning of Penal Code section 1192.7(c)(1)."

It is further alleged that in the commission and attempted commission of the above offense, the said defendant(s), ORENTHAL JAMES SIMPSON, personally used a deadly and dangerous weapon(s), to wit, knife, said use not being an element of the above offense, within the meaning of Penal Code section 12022(b) and also causing the above offense to be a serious felony within the meaning of Penal Code section 1192.7(c)(23).

* * * * *

It is further alleged as to Counts 1 and 2 the defendant has in this proceeding been convicted of more than one offense of murder in the first or second degree, within the meaning of Penal Code Section 190.2(a)(3).

Further, attached hereto and incorporated herein are official reports and documents of a law enforcement agency which the undersigned believes establish probable cause for the arrest of defendant(s) ORENTHAL JAMES SIMPSON, for the above-listed crimes. Wherefore, a warrant of arrest is requested for ORENTHAL JAMES SIMPSON.

I DECLARE UNDER PENALTY OF PERJURY THAT THE FOREGOING IS TRUE AND CORRECT AND THAT THIS COMPLAINT, CASE NUMBER BA097211 , CONSISTS OF 2 COUNT(S).

Executed at LOS ANGELES, County of Los Angeles, on June 17, 1994.

PHILLIP VANNATTER

DECLARANT AND COMPLAINANT

. . . .

GIL GARCETTI, DISTRICT ATTORNEY

BY:

MARCIA CLARK, DEPUTY

AGENCY: LAPD RHD | I/O: VANNATTER | ID NO: | PHONE NO: 485-2531

DR NO: 9408-17431 & 17432 | OPERATOR: | PRELIM.TIME EST.:

DEFENDANT	CII NO.	DOB	BOOKING NO.	BAIL RECOM'D	CUSTODY R'TN DATE
SIMPSON, ORENTHAL JAMES	M92188176	7/09/47		NO BAIL	

It appearing to the Court that probable cause exists for the issuance of a warrant of arrest for the above named defendant(s), the warrant is so ordered.

Judge of the above entitled Court

FELONY COMPLAINT - ORDER HOLDING TO ANSWER - P.C. SECTION 872

It appearing to me from the evidence presented that the following offense(s) has/have been committed and that there is sufficient cause to believe that the following defendant(s) guilty thereof, to wit:

(Strike out or add as applicable)

ORENTHAL JAMES SIMPSON

Count No.	Charge	Charge Range	Special Allegation	Alleg. Effect
1	PC187(a)	Check Code	PC12022(b)	+1 YR
2	PC187(a)	Check Code	PC12022(b)	+1 YR

I order that defendant(s) be held to answer therefor and be admitted to bail in the sum of:

ORENTHAL JAMES SIMPSON ______________________ Dollars

and be committed to the custody of the Sheriff of Los Angeles County until such bail is given. Date of arraignment in Superior Court will be:

ORENTHAL JAMES SIMPSON ______________ in Dept: ____

at: __________ A.M.

Date: ____________

____
Committing Magistrate

2.4

THE CALIFORNIA JURY SYSTEM

NUMBER OF JURORS

Although the U.S. Constitution has been interpreted to allow six person juries, Article I, Section 16 of the California Constitution guarantees 12 person juries for both felony and misdemeanor defendants. However, if all parties (prosecutor, defendant and the defense counsel) agree to waive this right, then a jury may consist of as few as six people. This rule is true for both felony and misdemeanor cases.[102]

THE JURY VERDICT AND JUROR SELECTION

Approximately 10% of all criminal cases heard in California courts by California juries end up as "hung" cases. One explanation for this may lie in the fact that criminal jury verdicts in California must by unanimous. The U.S. Constitution, on the other hand, does not prohibit non-unanimous jury verdicts. Various Federal constitutional cases have been decided by less than unanimous verdicts such as 9-3 and 10-2.[103]

Virtually all citizens ages 18 years and older residing in the jurisdiction in which they are summoned for duty are eligible to serve as jurors. Those who have prior felony convictions will be disqualified. Potential jurors are drawn from "master lists." Names included on the master list are taken from a variety of sources, including voter registrations, telephone directories, utility company lists, mailing lists, and records from the Department of Motor Vehicles.[104]

JURORS IN THE COURTROOM

In court, jurors are to take their task very seriously. Often, expectations of how jurors should conduct themselves in the courtroom are spelled out in written instructions. For example, such instructions have been prepared by the Committee on Standard Jury Instructions (Criminal) by the Superior Court of Los Angeles County (called "CALJIC"). These instructions provide a view as to what is expected of California's jurors. Jurors are instructed on how to take notes during trial (CALJIC 17.48), how to deliberate (CALJIC 17.40) and even how to maintain a proper attitude during their deliberations.[105]

DAILY PAY FOR JURY DUTY IN SELECTED STATES (1994)

Federal Jury	$40
Hawaii	$30
North Dakota	$25
Montana	$12
California	$ 5

Source: Sourcebook of Criminal Justice Statistics (1994)

2.5

TRIAL PROCEDURE AND PROPOSITION 115

Recently, various important changes in California courtroom procedures were introduced by the 1990 passage of Proposition 115, "The Crime Victim's Justice Reform Act." Many of these critical changes are presented below:

HERESAY EVIDENCE AT THE PRELIMINARY HEARING

First, this law changes the nature and stature of the preliminary hearing in California. Now, the prosecution, if they so choose, may use "hearsay" evidence at a preliminary hearing. This means that qualified officers may take the stand and relate information told to them by others. This hearsay procedure has impaired the defenses' ability to cross examine prosecution witnesses, and therefore has undermined some of the usefulness of the preliminary hearing to the defense.[106]

POST-INDICTMENT PRELIMINARY HEARINGS

Until recently, the California Supreme Court required that a preliminary hearing follow an indictment if the defendant so requests. This mandate in criminal procedure was destroyed by the passage of Prop 115. Thus, the grand jury indictment will no longer be a waste of time; if the grand jury chooses to hand down an indictment, the defendant must face the possibility of trial.[107]

"RECIPROCAL DISCOVERY"

Another notable product of Proposition 115 is "reciprocal discovery." California's reciprocal discovery provisions received national attention in the O.J. Simpson trial. This procedure involves both the prosecution and the defense exchanging information before the trial ever begins. The goal of these provisions is to avoid delay, gamesmanship and surprise in order to promote the truth finding function of trial. "Discovery" of some sort has always been a part of California's criminal justice process. The change produced by Prop 115 comes in the direction: Discovery is now a two-way street. Originally, the prosecution, within certain limits, had to provide the defense with the evidence it had gathered in its case against the defendant. Now, the defense must also provide information, such as names and statements of witnesses, test results, and tangible evidence. Sanctions for failure to abide by reciprocal discovery provisions include delaying witness' testimony, allowing continuances and admonishing the jurors.[108]

PLEA BARGAINING

Another difference in California's pretrial procedure occurs during plea bargaining. Plea bargaining is now forbidden for certain crimes, including "serious felonies" (including murder, voluntary manslaughter, mayhem and rape), felonies involving personal use of a firearm, or driving under the influence. Critics of this procedural change introduced by Prop 115 have argued that a strict reading of this statute would dramatically increase the number of trials and create a huge case backlog in California courts. However, in practice, many court have devised procedural methods to cope with increasing case loads due to restrictions placed on plea bargaining.[109]

VOIR DIRE

At the trial itself, among the most interesting features in California procedure is the *voir dire* process. "Voir dire," means literally "to speak the truth." It is the process by which the trial jury is selected (by the judge, prosecution and defense) from a pool of potential jurors. It's primary purpose is to screen prospective jurors for biases regarding matter relating to the specifics of the case and the defendant(s). After the passage of Prop 115, California's new law places the control of voir dire proceedings in the hands of the trial judge. Now, judges have several options as to how they will structure the *voir dire* proceedings. On the one hand, a judge may choose to allow *voir dire* to proceed as it did before Prop 115 (i.e., allow attorneys to directly ask the jurors as many questions as they wish). On the other hand, the judge may do one of several other things, including: (1) limiting the number of the questions introduced in a *voir dire* session; (2) becoming the mouthpiece for attorneys by asking the prospective jurors questions for the attorneys; or (3) rejecting totally attorneys' requests to question potential jurors, allowing only questions and questioning to be conducted by the judge.

The aim of this change by Prop 115 was to emulate the Federal *voir dire* process in hopes of shortening the length of trials. Concern is sometimes voiced that judicial *voir dire* may be less probing, and therefore may fail to detect certain jurors who may improperly influence a verdict or "hang" a jury.[110]

ACQUITTAL RATES FOR CALIFORNIA JURY AND COURT TRIALS

	JURY	COURT
1987	18.1%	24.6%
1988	17.3%	27.7%
1989	16.8%	21.1%
1990	17.8%	20.3%
1991	18.8%	20.7%

Source: Judicial Council of California (1995)

2.6

SENTENCING

ADULT SENTENCING

Throughout most of California's history, the sentencing of adult convicted offenders has been handled in an "indeterminate" manner. That is, sentences prescribed by law for a given criminal offense specified a minimum and maximum term (i.e., 15 years to life). The primary goal underlying California's "indeterminate" sentencing method was rehabilitation of the offender by the Department of Corrections. In keeping with this philosophy, the state authorized the Department of Corrections (through its parole function) to determine an inmate's release time depending on "when he or she was deemed fit to return to society."[111]

During the late 1960's and on into the early 1970's, California's long-standing method of "indeterminate" sentencing came under severe scrutiny and criticism from police, citizens, elected officials, inmates and judges. Law enforcement viewed the system as too lenient, resulting in the unwarranted early release of violent offenders. Inmates were displeased because they felt that indeterminate sentences resulted in giving corrections officials too much "political" control over inmates. For the first time in the history of the California criminal justice system, there was unanimous agreement among law enforcement, courts and corrections officials that "indeterminate sentencing must go." [112]

In the mid-1970's and later, a series of laws introduced into the Assembly by Senator Robert Presley resulted in the replacement of California's "indeterminate" sentences with "determinate" sentences. Thus, criminals who are now sentenced under California law receive what's commonly referred to as "flat time." In effect, this shift in the state's sentencing methods represented a clear philosophical move away from rehabilitation to punishment.[113]

Instead of prescribing a minimum and maximum term, the Penal Code now stipulates three specific terms for most crimes: a low term, a medium term and a high term. When sentenced, most offenders will receive the average or "medium" term. There must be "mitigating" circumstances surrounding a particular case to receive a lower term (i.e., first-time, non-violent offense) and "aggravated" circumstances to receive a high term (i.e., use of a weapon, injury to a victim). Specific indeterminate sentences are still given for a few extremely violent offenses (e.g., first-degree murder).[114]

Most important, however, the decision making power and discretion once held by the corrections officials regarding the length of sentence has now been shifted to the prosector. Thus, it is up to the prosecution (and the specific charges they seek) and not the Department of Corrections regarding how much time an adult offender will ultimately serve in prison.[115]

JUVENILE SENTENCING

The focus of the juvenile justice system is not on punishment, but rather on reforming the behavior of juveniles by promoting rehabilitation and deterrence. Hence, juvenile justice is an entirely separate system from the adult system. Minors who find themselves in juvenile court are treated much differently than their adult counterparts. Minors have no right to a jury trial, and thus their cases are heard instead behind closed doors in front of a single judge. Juveniles who are found to be "involved" in delinquent conduct are "recommended" to sentences that are based on the seriousness of the crime(s) they have committed. However, these sentences may not exceed those of "flat time" sentences for comparable crimes committed by adults.[117]

Certain juveniles are considered unable to benefit from the juvenile justice system, which focuses on rehabilitation. These minors have been found, in "fitness hearings" under Welfare and Institutions Code (WIC) 707, to "not be amenable to the care, treatment and training program available through the facilities of the juvenile court..." This is based upon an evaluation of one or more of the following factors: (1) the degree of the minor's criminal sophistication, (2) whether the minor can be rehabilitated before expiration of the juvenile court's jurisdiction, (3) the minor's previous delinquent history, (4) the juvenile court's previous success is in rehabilitating the minor, and (5) the circumstances and gravity of the offense. If these factors weigh against the juvenile, he or she will be found "unfit" for the juvenile system and certified to adult court.[117]

SELECTED OFFENSES AND PENAL CODE TERMS FOR ADULT OFFENDERS

Offense	"Low"	"Medium"	"High"
Murder (Spec. Circ.)*	Life w/out parole or death		
Murder (1st Degree)	25 to life		
Murder (2nd Degree)**	15 to life		
Kidnap	5yrs.	8yrs.	11yrs.
Robbery (1st Degree)	3yrs.	4yrs.	6yrs.
Robbery (2nd Degree)	2yrs.	3yrs.	5yrs.
Assault (Aggravated)	2yrs.	3yrs.	4yrs.
Burglary (1st Degree)	2yrs.	4yrs.	6yrs.

* Special circumstances must be proven

** If police officer, 25 to life; from motor vehicle, 20 to life.

2.7

SENTENCING ALTERNATIVES

RESTITUTION

Many have criticized the criminal courts for focusing their attention almost exclusively on the defendants; litigation in this area of the law centers around what the accused did or thought, or what actions law enforcement took against the criminal. Further, district and city attorneys, prosecuting "public offenses," are mindful that they represent all the people in the state (rather than the victim).

Decisions on how to proceed with a particular criminal matter are generally out of the victim's hands. Moreover, lost time at work, high parking fees, long delays without explanation and even rude attorneys can cause victims to feel mistreated and forgotten. As part of an effort to interject the interests of victims in the criminal justice process, California enacted Penal Code 1202.4, a statute which orders defendants to pay to victims costs incurred as a result of the criminal's actions. However, the practical effect of this law may be somewhat limited because many defendants do not have the ability to pay the amount of restitution to victims which is ordered by the court.[118]

DIVERSION

California has recognized that not all people who violate the law are proper candidates for traditional criminal prosecution. Indeed, there is a fear that processing some individuals through the system may even harden them into nonproductive members of society. Therefore, California has created, in PC 1000.1 to 1000.5, the option of "diversion."

According to these statutes, eligible individuals may be "diverted" out of the criminal justice system, and their cases will be frozen while they pursue a rehabilitation program designed to educate and reform. If the defendant successfully completes the program, "the arrest upon which the diversion was based shall be deemed to have never occurred." However, should the defendant fail to satisfactorily complete the program, criminal proceedings shall be resumed. Thus, diversion provides certain people who find themselves in the midst of a criminal prosecution a final opportunity to undo their mistake and avoid criminal sanctions.[119]

THE VICTIM OFFENDER RECONCILIATION PROGRAM

The two preceding options of restitution and diversion are built-in as part of California's criminal justice system. They are also vulnerable to some of the harmful effects of "the system" such as inefficiency and delay. Because of these and other problems linked to over-worked and over-crowded courts, there has been a recent move in California to address criminal behavior with programs entirely outside of the traditional system.

One example of this approach is offered by The Victim Offender Reconciliation Program (VORP). This program provides the victim and offender the opportunity to meet directly to resolve issues created by the criminal's wrongful acts. If both the victim and the wrongdoer agree to participate in the program, they meet in the presence of a VORP case worker in order to negotiate a contract.

Under the terms of their agreement, the offenders obligate themselves to perform certain tasks in order to compensate the victim for any loss. Failure to live up to the contract triggers re-initiation of criminal proceedings. It is hoped that, by working out their own resolution, both the victim and offender may reach a more satisfactory and lasting result than that offered by the traditional court system.[120]

Pictured above: The L.A. County Criminal Courts Building, which has been the center of many of the nation's most visible cases, including O.J. Simpson, Rodney King, the Menendez Brothers, the McMartin Pre-School, the "Night Stalker" and many other notable cases.

2.8

THE STREET TERRORISM ENFORCEMENT AND PREVENTION ACT (STEP)

California has the dubious distinction of being the home to the nation's most violent criminal gangs. In 1988, the California legislature responded to the dangers caused by these gangs by passing a law commonly referred to as the "STEP Act" (Street Terrorism Enforcement and Prevention Act). According to California Penal Code Section 186.22(a), violations and punishments outlined by the STEP Act[121] are as follows:

"Any person who actively participates in a criminal street gang with knowledge that the gang's members engage in or have engaged in a pattern of criminal activity and who willfully promotes, furthers, or assists in any felonious criminal conduct by members of that gangs shall be punished by imprisonment in the county jail for a period not to exceed one year or in state prison for one, two or three years."[122]

In practice, the above law makes active participation in a criminal street gang, along with willful promotion of felonious criminal conduct, a felony. In creating this law, the state was specifically targeting for criminal prosecution people who participate in criminal street gangs. However, gang participation alone is not deemed a criminal act according to this law. In addition, the STEP Act provides a detailed definition of a criminal street gang as "...an ongoing organization, association or group of three or more persons whether formal or informal:

A. Having as one of its primary activities the commission of one or more of the following:
   1. ADW (assault with a deadly weapon)
   2. Robbery
   3. Homicide or Manslaughter
   4. Sale or Possession for Sale of Narcotics
   5. Shooting Inhabited Dwelling or Car
   6. Arson
   7. Witness Intimidation;

B. which has a common name or common identifying sign or symbol;
C. whose members individually or collectively engage in or have engaged in a pattern of criminal gang activity.[123]

Since the STEP Act provides a detailed definition of a "criminal street gang," not every "gang" will fall under this law. Among other things, a "criminal street gang" must have as one of its "primary activities" the commission of one or more of the felonies listed in this law. Other sections of the STEP Act create authorization (1) to declare buildings used by criminal street gang members "nuisances" subject to court injunctions, (2) to provide for sentencing enhancements for certain felonies committed to benefit a gang, and (3) to define the crime of "terrorist threats."

2.9

SPECIAL PROSECUTORIAL PROGRAMS

THREE STRIKES

In 1994, Section 667 of the California Penal Code was amended to include a "three strikes" provision. This law works in three stages. In the first stage, if a person commits either a "serious felony" or a "violent felony" he or she will receive the normal sentence for this first offense. Serious and violent felonies include crimes such as:

> murder, voluntary manslaughter, mayhem, rape, arson and selling certain controlled substances to minors.[124]

The second stage of the three strikes law occurs upon the commission of a second offense. Here, if the accused has one prior conviction for either a serious or violent felony, and then commits **any** felony, his or her prison term will be doubled. In the third stage, when a criminal possesses two priors of either serious or violent felonies, and then commits **any** felony, he or she is sentenced to 25 years to life (with very few opportunities to obtain early release).[125]

The "three strikes" law has been criticized for being too broad because the second and third stages may be triggered by the defendant's commission of **any** felony, including those that are neither serious nor violent. The law has also been blamed for clogging California's court system because now only a small fraction of defendants possessing one or two prior "strikes" are willing to forego their trial in exchange for a plea bargain. Critics of the law have also claimed that excessive crowding of county jails and state correctional facilities is also a direct result of having to house "three strikes" inmates for longer periods of time.[126]

LA COUNTY ENVIRONMENTAL CRIMES STRIKE FORCE

The Los Angeles County Environmental Crimes Strike Force was first implemented in the early 1980's. While the District Attorney's Office has assumed the lead role in "Strike Force" prosecutions of environmental crimes (e.g., unlawful hazardous materials disposal and unlicensed transporters), other agencies play important roles as well. Strike force membership includes local, state and county law enforcement; city and county public works departments; city and county sanitation districts; and the South Coast Air Quality Management District. Although the district attorney's office has both civil and criminal jurisdiction, deputy prosecutors use civil proceedings only when criminal remedies are unavailable. Strike Force attorneys view criminal prosecution as a more effective deterrent than administrative or civil proceedings. Criminal prosecution is generally faster than the civil route, and the fines and penalties obtainable through criminal prosecution are as large or larger than the available civil remedies. Moreover, prosecutors in Los Angeles County have crafted criminal penalties that make cleanup of a site or remeditation of an environmental problem a condition of probation.[127]

THE RIVERSIDE COUNTY STREET ENFORCEMENT AND PREVENTION PROGRAM

The Riverside County Street Enforcement and Prevention Program was derived from California's STEP Act. The Riverside County District Attorneys' Office has developed written notices, for service by police officers on gang members, which state that a specific gang is considered a criminal street gang under the STEP Act and that participation in the gang can subject an individual to a sentence of one to three years. The Riverside Police Department, under the guidance of the county prosecutor, has undertaken an elaborate process for compiling intelligence on gangs, which facilitates linking of individuals to specific gangs. Preservation of the record of notification served by police on suspected gang members destroys any claim that a defendant did not know of the street gang's criminal activity.[128]

SAN DIEGO COUNTY'S FAMILY PROTECTION DIVISION

The San Diego County District Attorney's Office has had a longstanding commitment to the prosecution of physical abuse of children cases, as well as sexual abuse cases, illustrated by its distinction as one of the first in the country to prosecute a parent for an injury that was caused because a child was not placed in an infant car seat. The Family Protection Division within the district attorney's office was conceived in 1985. All felony cases of abuse of children under 14 years of age are prosecuted in the Family Protection Division. Deputies are provided with highly specialized training. Law enforcement officers are encouraged to consult with prosecutors regarding evidentiary matters before making an arrest in any child abuse case. The specialization within the district attorney's office has created a unit of professionals highly knowledgeable in key areas such as the psychology of child abusers, the dynamics of intrafamilial abuse, and explanation of medical findings for injuries.[129]

3.1

CALIFORNIA JAILS

THE STATE'S FIRST JAILS

Pre-Gold Rush

Jails did not become a fixture of California's landscape until after the gold rush of 1849. Prior to this time, there was little need to construct permanent detention facilities for offenders because crime and criminals were relatively rare within early California communities.

Historical records indicate that few jails existed during this time period, and those that did were used exclusively to house offenders awaiting trial and never used to house criminals as a means of punishment.[130] The largest of these "jails" (circa 1835) was located in the village of *Yerba Buena*, which later became the City of San Francisco. The following inventory list, obtained from the *Yerba Buena* jailer's log,[131] illustrates the primitive nature of California's earliest jails:

o 1 serviceable padlock
o 2 chairs
o 1 pair of shackles which are missing and should be searched for in passing

Post-Gold Rush

The discovery of gold in California brought with it rapid social, economic and legal change. Crime was also an unfortunate by-product of the gold rush. With prospectors arriving from both the eastern states and abroad to seek overnight wealth, the chaotic "wild west" became a haven for thieves, robbers, murderers and other serious law breakers.[132]

In order to counter California's first crime wave, citizens demanded that secure facilities be created within local police jurisdictions to hold accused offenders. In 1849, the County of San Francisco established the first permanent jail in California. The jail, which was actually a "hulk," consisted of a two-masted brig named *The Euphemia*. The floating jail was anchored a short distance off the San Francisco coast.[133]

Around this same time, other California cities and counties began to copy the San Francisco "jail" model. Sacramento purchased a ship named the *La Grange* to use as its regional jail. In Los Angeles, the first jail consisted of an adobe residence wherein accused offenders were chained to a pine log. Contra Costa County constructed a small stone jail. The first jail in Auburn was a log cabin. The Calusa County Jail consisted of an iron cage that was moved in the shade of a tree by a Justice of the Peace.[134]

CONTEMPORARY CALIFORNIA JAILS

The Nation's Largest System of Jails

Many critics argue that the living conditions in the modern California jails are no better, or perhaps even worse, than those which characterized the gold rush era. However, the fact that California has the nation's (and possibly the world's) largest and most complex jail system cannot be denied. There are approximately 131 major jails in California with an average daily inmate population of about 75,000 inmates. Roughly one out of every five persons who is in a U.S. jail is serving time behind bars in a California jail.[135]

Most jails in California are operated at the county level, administered by the County Sheriff and staffed by Sheriff's Deputies. Some, however, are maintained at the city level by local police. These smaller, more temporary facilities are referred to as "lock-ups."

California Jails in Transition

Presently, however, the California jail system (at least in larger cities) appears to be in transition. There is clearly a move by many counties to create "corrections departments" which operate jails independently of county law enforcement functions. Throughout the state this is referred to as the "Santa Clara Model." This is because during the 1980's the Santa Clara County Sheriff's Department was the first to pioneer the idea of staffing their jail with permanent "corrections officers" rather than Sheriff's Deputies. The model has proven to be very effective because, among other things, it allows more deputies to work the streets (who would otherwise work in the jail).[136]

Jails appear to be changing physically as well. Many of California's older, larger jails were built in the early 1900's and are literally crumbling to pieces. These decaying jails are being replaced with "new generation" jails such as the L.A. County's "Twin Towers" jail, designed to hold 4000 maximum security inmates, and the Presley Center in Riverside County.

THE LARGEST JAIL SYSTEM IN THE WORLD: L.A. COUNTY

Originally built to hold some 12,000 inmates, the L.A. County jail system now consists of eight separate jails which together hold around 20,000 inmates. During the 1992 riots, the L.A. County jail system swelled to over 25,000 inmates. The cost to house one inmate for one year in this system is approximately $15,000.[137]

The largest of L.A. County's jails is the Men's Central Jail located in the heart of downtown Los Angeles. Men's Central Jail is the largest single jail facility in the world. It has an average daily population of around 6,000 inmates. About 250,000 persons are processed through this facility each year. Only 165 unarmed deputies (about 7% of which are female) staff the jail on any given shift. Approximately 18,000 inmate meals are served each day and the jail's laundry facility maintains 27,000 sets of inmate clothing.[138]

Pictured above: Los Angeles County Men's Central Jail

The Men's Central Jail inmate population is quite diverse, consisting of the nation's most violent felons as well as Hollywood's biggest stars. Some of the facility's more famous inmates include O.J. Simpson, Sean Penn, Christian Brando (son of actor Marlon Brando), Richard Ramirez (The Night Stalker), Sirhan Sirhan (assassin of Sen. Robert Kennedy), Charles Manson, Angelo Buono (The Hillside Strangler) and many other "high profile" individuals.

The jail also operates a program called "Operation Safe Jails" (O.S.J) which provides specially trained deputies and specialized facilities to deal with known gang inmates. Within the jail there is one isolated group of cells referred to as "the gang module" consisting of separate wings where members of the rival gangs "Crips" and "Bloods" are housed. In addition, there is also a unit called "High Power" which consists of one-man cells holding extremely dangerous inmates. Most "High Power" inmates are segregated from the general jail population because they have been identified as "shot callers" (i.e., inmates who are highly influential over other inmates) such as prison gang leaders.

COURT CASES AFFECTING CALIFORNIA JAIL OPERATIONS

Although there are thousands of laws that affect the operation of California's jail, listed below are results from several court cases that directly impact state jail administration:

1. Block v. Rutherford (1984) 104 S. Ct. 3227

This case began as a class action suit against the Los Angeles County Sheriff's Department and concerned the operation of its Men's Central Jail. The following are key policy changes in jail operations resulting from the decision of this case.

o Clothing Each inmate must receive clean clothing and a towel at least twice per week.

o Sleeping Inmates must be provided a "reasonable" amount of sleep.

o Beds Every inmate must have a bunk and mattress to sleep on. Any inmate who must sleep on the floor due to an emergency must have a mattress and bedding.

o Meals Every inmate must have at least 15 minutes to eat.

o Recreation Televisions must be placed inside each dayroom. All inmates except high security, discipline or hospitalized inmates must receive at least 2 hours of outdoor exercise each week. Stationary bicycles must be provided for inmates not able to receive outdoor exercise.

2. Bell v. Wolfish (1979) 441 U.S. 529

This case established that the jail administrator can create policy without court intervention as long as a rational or reasonable basis exists for the policy. Policies are judged as "reasonable" if the jail administrator's interests in maintaining security in the jail outweigh the requests or rights of the inmates.

3. Wolff v. Mc Donnell (1974) 418 U.S. 539

The U.S. Supreme Court held in this case that the discipline procedures used by correctional personnel must comply with due process requirements, with certain limits. The inmate must receive notice of the violation, time to prepare and present a defense, an impartial hearing officer and the right to appeal. Witnesses can be called only if relevant and do not present a security hazard.

4. Hudson v. Palmer (1984) 104 U.S. 3194

This U.S. Supreme Court decision stipulated that an inmate has no right to privacy in his jail cell. Jail staff do not need a reason, probable cause or, a warrant to search. However, the search must be for security reasons or to find contraband, not to harass or "punish" an inmate.

5. Robertson v. Block 82 1442 WPG (Px)

This case essentially required jail staff to segregate homosexual inmates from heterosexual inmates. However, equal consideration must be given to homosexual inmates for visiting, education, medical treatment and other basic inmate rights and privileges.

PENAL CODE SECTIONS AFFECTING JAIL OPERATIONS

The manner in which California jail personnel handle inmates is governed not only by case law, but also by penal code statutes. Improper care of inmates by jail staff can result in criminal as well as civil sanctions. The following are examples of penal code provisions which are applicable to those who are charged with the care and custody of inmates in California:

673 P.C. Cruel, Corporal or Unusual Punishment

Anyone who subjects any inmate or prisoner to cruel or unusual treatment or punishment, or who allows any lack of care that would injure the health of an inmate, or anyone who aids, abets or contributes to such treatment is guilty of a misdemeanor.

149 P.C. Officer Unnecessarily Assaulting or Beating any Person

Any officer who, under color of authority beats or assaults any person without lawful necessity can be punished by a fine of up to $10,000 and be imprisoned in the state prison or in the county jail for up to one year.

Pictured above: L.A. County's "new generation" jail--Twin Towers.

JAILS FOR YOUTHS: JUVENILE HALL

Persons under 18 years of age in California who are taken into legal custody are "detained" in juvenile hall. These detention facilities for minors were first located within each of California's counties in 1909 and are today supervised and staffed by each county's probation department. Activities and operations of juvenile hall are monitored by the county Juvenile Court and by the California Youth Authority.[139]

The primary function of juvenile hall is detention. For the most part, they are used to house youths before, during and after adjudication (or trial). In 1994, juvenile hall throughout California housed some 15,000 youths. There are twice as many minors in California's juvenile hall than in any other state.[140]

The most serious problem facing California's juvenile halls is the changing nature of their offender populations. Because the majority of the state's juvenile detention facilities were constructed during the 1950's, 60's or 70's to house minor offenders, they are not equipped or staffed to hand the recent influx of violent offenders of the 1990's.

Security is a serious issue in today's California juvenile halls and to those who staff these facilities. Within the last several years, many counties have experienced serious juvenile custody problems. For example, in Yolo County, nine detainees knocked out a counselor with a barbell to stage their escape.

In Los Angeles' Central Juvenile Hall (the largest in the nation), a car was used to slam into the gates of an exercise yard to carry out an escape. In Fresno, an escape was carried out by holding a probation officer at gun point. In San Joaquin County, wards in juvenile hall staged a violent escape where they sliced off a counselor's nose with the leg of a ping-pong table to gain access to master control to their holding area. In the last four years, more than 100 juvenile detainees have escaped from San Francisco's Youth Guidance Center.[141]

Situations such as those described above have prompted county officials to "beef up" security in California's juvenile halls. Of particular concern to officials is how to handle the custody of juveniles who are being tried in adult courts. These "hardcore" juvenile offenders pose especially serious custody risks to detention staff, and to other youths who are being detained.

It is not uncommon for youths who are being tried as adults to require one or two years in juvenile hall before their case is resolved. Legislators in California have proposed that such offenders be housed in county jails along with adults. However, the existing law still requires that minors be segregated from adults or at least out of sight and sound of them.[142]

3.2

CALIFORNIA PRISONS

THE BEGINNING OF THE PRISON "SYSTEM"

Shortly after California achieved statehood in 1850, the state's early system of local jails came under extreme scrutiny and criticism. Generally speaking, the public felt that jails were unsafe for inmates as well as the community. For the inmate, disease and death resulting from inadequate food, exercise and sanitation were likely to result from being placed in custody.[143] On the other hand, numerous incidents of attacks on citizens by hardened criminals who had escaped from confinement further fueled the public's intolerance of local jails.[144] State officials soon found an answer California's jail problem: the prison.

Ironically, California's first jail was a "hulk" and so was its first temporary prison; in fact, they were both the created by using the same vessel (*The Euphemia*). After purchasing *The Euphemia* from the County of San Francisco, Generals M.G. Vallejo and James M. Estell entered into a contact with the State of California to "lease" its prisons. Under the care and custody of Vallejo and Estell, the prisoners labored by day to profit for their keepers. At night all inmates were shackled within small, filthy quarters located beneath the deck of *The Euphemia.*[145]

The name given to the floating prison was *Corte Madera State Prison* (Spanish translation: "The Wooden Court," which was later transformed into San Quentin Prison). Its population consisted of 82 men and one woman. California's first female inmate, whose name is believed to have been "Scottish Mary," was housed along with her male counterparts. She was serving a sentence of one year from San Francisco County for assisting in the escape of a prisoner.[146]

THE EARLY SYSTEM: A SYSTEM OF SEPARATE PRISONS

San Quentin State Prison (1852): California's First Prison

Several significant events took place in 1852 which shaped the future of California's penal system. First, within a relatively short period of time, California's first prison was drastically overcrowded. With an inmate population of 150 men and three women, the State's prison ship was filled to nearly four times its capacity.

To accommodate the tremendous influx of new inmates, the State purchased a piece of land where a larger, more permanent correctional facility could be constructed. The land purchased was Point Quentin, located on the tip of the San Francisco Bay, for a sum of $10,000. Several sources allege that the original owner of this land was none other than General Estell, the "lessee" and "warden" of California's inmates.[147]

The construction of *San Quentin State Prison*, known today by inmates as the "Q," began immediately following the State's purchase of Point Quentin. Estell, the businessman that he was, worked a deal with state officials to supply all construction labor for the project. To do so, he merely beached his overcrowded "hulk" at the construction site and used *his* inmates to build *their* own prison. Needless to say, Estell profited handsomely as the "foreman" of this project.[148] The first cell block was completed and occupied in 1854, about two years after construction began. The building had no plumbing, lights or heat. The only light available to inmates was from a small slot in the large iron door that covered the entrance to each inmate's cell. Eventually, a few gas lamps were installed to light walkways for guards who patrolled the cell block at night. This original cell block (called "The Stone House") was used to house inmates until 1959.[149]

San Quentin is still fully operational today, and it is the oldest prison in the California Department of Corrections System. It is perhaps best known for being the home of "condemned row," where all males who have been sentenced to death reside. It is also the location of California's gas chamber. According to contemporary law, all state executions (for male and female inmates) must be carried out at San Quentin. California's first "Boot Camp" for inmates was also established at San Quentin in the early 1990's.

Folsom State Prison (1880): California's Second Prison

Not long after the prison at San Quentin was opened it became severely overcrowded. This prompted the search for a site where a second prison could be built. Approximately 25 miles northeast of Sacramento, a site was discovered that was not only close to major railroads and but rich with natural granite deposits. Here, the ground was broken for California's second prison--*Folsom State Prison.* Like its predecessor, Folsom was build by inmates who were leased by the State to perform the construction for a private contractor.[150] Granite boulders from nearby quarries were fashioned by inmates into cellblocks which were occupied in 1880.

As will be discussed later, Folsom and San Quentin were both authorized to carry out executions in the name of the state. The method of execution, until the early 1940's was hanging. A total of 92 inmates died in Folsom's gallows. In fact, California's last official inmate hanging was held on May 1, 1942 at Folsom. California executions were no longer held at Folsom after death by lethal gas replaced the gallows in the late 1930's.[151]

Folsom prison is still California's second oldest functioning prison. However, the institution and its inmate population have undergone many changes since its early years. For example, Folsom's reputation for housing the state's "toughest and most dangerous" inmates is no longer valid. Folsom is now used to house relatively low risk offenders. High risk offenders are now kept in more modern institutions which are equipped with the latest "high tech" facilities.

Tehachapi Women's Prison (1933): California's First Women's Prison

In the mid-1920's there was growing discussion within the California Legislature regarding what to do with the state's female inmates. During this time, all females sentenced to serve time in prison were housed in a special wing above the Administration Building at San Quentin. There was considerable talk about how the small population of inmate women (around 30-50) was mistreated and

In the early 1930s, an isolated site near the town of Tehachapi was selected as the home of California's first prison exclusively for women. The doors of the facility first opened in 1933. All of California's female inmate population was transported from San Quentin to the new facility, which was originally named "California Institution for Women." The purpose of the institution was for the "confinement, care, reformation of women misdemeanants convicted of a felony the punishment for which is less than death." CIW was run in a reformatory style, and its first inmate population consisted of women considered to be either "drug addicts or vagrants."[153]

Pictured above: The main entrance to the California Institution for Women in Frontera.

Due to earthquake damage, bad weather conditions and an isolated location, CIW was closed and replaced in 1952 by a newer facility located in Frontera, also known today as "California Institution for Women." The Tehachapi facility was reopened in 1954 under the name "California Correctional Institution," which is still operational today.[154]

California Institution for Men (1941): California's Third Prison

As California's population began to shift from the north to the south, there became a critical need to augment San Quentin and Folsom with a third institution located somewhere in Southern California. The large, and desolate, agricultural region near the town of Chino was selected as this next prison site. The prison was opened in 1941 under the original name of "Southern California Prison." Its mission was to provide "confinement, discipline, instruction and training of first time offenders between the ages of 18 and 24....who in the judgement of the court were capable of reformation." Thus, unlike San Quentin or Folsom, CIM was viewed by its creators as a "reformatory" for a different, less hardened, type of offender.[155]

Ironically, the present day mission of CIM is not much different from its original mission. CIW is still considered one of California's largest "minimum" security institutions. It also serves as classification center for inmates who are first entering the system.

Soledad State Prison (1946): California's First Medical Prison

Soledad State Prison was designed as California's first "medical prison." Located in the central portion of the state, this prison was originally constructed to house inmates who were "mentally ill, defective, epileptic, addicted to narcotics, sex offenders or suffered from chronic disease."[156]

Today, Soledad prison houses a general inmate population, rather than "special" inmate population which requires particular medical or psychiatric attention. The medical function of Soledad was later replaced by the California Medical Facility located in Vacaville (where Charles Manson and other "special" inmates have been assigned).

THE ROOTS OF CALIFORNIA'S CORRECTIONAL SYSTEM

Under one central administration, the California Department of Corrections, the state's prison system rapidly expanded during the 1950's and 60's. Prisons built during this period included the following:

o California Institution for Women (1952): Frontera

o Duel Vocational Institution (1953): Tracy

o California Correctional Institution (1954): Tehachapi

o California Men's Colony (1954): San Luis Obispo

o California Medical Facility (1955): Vacaville

o California Rehabilitation Center (1962): Norco

7. California Correctional Center (1963): Susanville

8. Sierra Conservation Center (1965): Jamestown

The institutions listed above, along with San Quentin, Folsom, CIM and Soledad, comprised the entire California Department of Corrections until 1984.[157]

CORRECTIONS IN CALIFORNIA TODAY

Today's system of corrections in California is complex, and the largest of its kind in the world. Persons convicted of crimes in California are handled in a variety of ways and in a variety of separate systems existing at the state, county and local levels.

In California, as a general rule, convicted offenders are referred to local or county correctional agencies if they have been sentenced to one year or less; or they have been sentenced to an "intermediate" sanction such as probation, restitution, community service and so forth. These classes of offenders usually include misdemeanants and persons who are first-time offenders who have committed low-grade felonies.

Felons who have received sentences of more than one year are referred to the state correctional system. Adults, i.e., usually persons 18 years of age or older, serve their time in the California Department of Corrections (known as "CDC"). Serious offenders under the age of 18 years who have not been tried as an "adult" are referred to the California Youth Authority (known as "CYA"). Both the Department of Corrections and the Youth Authority are branches of the Youth and Adult Correctional Agency, which oversees the administration of all state correctional agencies.

Pictured above: The entrance to California State Institution for Men (CIM).

Source: California Department of Corrections (1994)

3.3

CALIFORNIA DEPARTMENT OF CORRECTIONS

According to the California Penal Code, the stated purpose of the California Department of Corrections (CDC) is "punishment." The CDC operates all state prisons for adult men and women. A state-wide system of 38 conservation camps known as "Prisons Without Walls" is also operated by the CDC. In addition, the CDC oversees the operations of numerous community correctional facilities such as halfway houses and clinics. The CDC is also responsible for the administration and operations of the state adult parole system. Supervision, surveillance and other specialized services for parolees are provided by the CDC.[158]

INSTITUTIONS OR PRISONS

Prison Expansion. Currently, the CDC operates 29 prisons throughout the state. However, this number has been and will be increasing rapidly. Prior to 1982, there were only 12 original prisons to serve the state's entire inmate population. During the past decade, the CDC has added 40,524 prison cells and dormitory beds by building 16 new prisons and renovating other ones. By the turn of the century it is estimated the entire CDC system will have somewhere between 55 and 60 prisons in its system.[159]

Inmate Population. The present inmate population under supervision by the CDC is about 127,000 persons. Of these persons, approximately 117,000 are confined to institutions. This represents a dramatic increase from the CDC's inmate population of 1980, which was just under 30,000. Unfortunately, state prisons become overcrowded just as soon as they are built. The "three strikes" legislation is the most recent of some 1,100 "get tough on crime" changes that have been made to the California Penal Code over the past 15 years. The existing prisons are designed to house 66,000 inmates, one to each cell. However, almost all cells are double bunked. California's inmate population is expected to climb to around 230,000.[160]

Costs. During the past decade, the state's prison budget grew from less than $730 million per year to about $3.1 billion in 1995. The cost to construct an average CDC institution, which is designed to house about 4,000 medium security inmates, is $200,000 million. The most expensive institution was the "supermax" facility located at Pelican Bay, which cost $240,000 million in 1989. For a maximum security institution, construction costs average $113,000 per cell; for minimum security institutions the cell cost is $60,000. It costs an average of $21,000 per year to house one inmate. California's prisons cost around $75 million per year to operate. Construction and expansion of CDC institutions have been financed largely through a series of voter approved bond initiatives.[161]

Inmate Characteristics. Most inmates housed within CDC institutions are male (93.5%). By race, the majority are Hispanic (33.8%) followed by African-Americans (32.1%), Caucasians (29.2%) and other races (4.9%). The majority are serving time for a violent offense (42.4%). Property and drug offenders respectively comprise 26% and 25% of the total inmate population. On average, inmates are 31 years of age and read at the eighth grade level. Their average sentence is 41 months.[162]

CDC Officers and Staff. The motto of CDC officers is "we walk the toughest beat in the state." The 22,500 sworn CDC officers represent the largest law enforcement organization in California and the second largest in the United States (second only to the City of New York, which has roughly 30,000 sworn officers). Line officers must complete a six week residential academy located in Galt (near Sacramento). CDC officers are sworn peace officers who must be trained in numerous mental and physical defense skills as well as in the operations of numerous firearms such as the Ruger Mini-14, H&K Model 94 and the Remington 870 12-gauge shotgun. Nearly all of the 15,000 non-sworn CDC staff employees are hired from the ranks of professions such as psychology, medicine, education, engineering, law and business administration. Because the CDC is a self-contained community, there is a need to hire staff in nearly every trade and service industry as well.[163]

S.E.R.T. Each prison has a highly trained unit referred to as SERT (Special Emergency Response Team). They are similar in function to a police department's SWAT team. SERT teams respond to emergency situations within the prison and their members are experts in emergency tactics such as hostage negotiation, crisis management and the tactical use of specialized weapons.[164]

Health Care. Inmates requiring health care must be treated within a CDC facility. Four licensed hospitals, complete with their own medical staff, are maintained by the CDC. The newest and largest hospital is located at Corcoran, with the other three being located at the California Medical Facility (Vacaville), California Men's Colony (San Luis Obispo), and the California Institution for Men (Chino). The Central California Women's Facility (Chowchilla) has recently opened a licensed "Skilled Nursing Facility" for women. In addition, all prisons maintain an on-site infirmary and dental clinic.[165]

HOW INMATES ARE PROCESSED THROUGH THE CDC

1. The Reception Center

Shortly after being convicted, adult felons are transported from county jail by the CDC to one of the Department's regional reception centers. These centers serve as the point of entry into the correctional system for the newly convicted offender, and they are where the offender's initial classification is performed.

There are separate reception centers for men and women, and for offenders sentenced in northern, central and southern California. Northern reception centers for men are located in San Francisco (San Quentin) and Tracy (Deuel Vocational Institution). Male offenders are received in the

State's central area at Wasco and Delano. Southern California male reception centers are located in Chino (California Institution for Men) and San Diego (R.J. Donovan Correctional Facility). Women are received at the Central California Women's Facility in Chowchilla and the Northern California Women's Facility in Stockton. Offenders with critical mental or physical impairments are received at the California Medical Facility in Vacaville.[166]

2. Classification

California prisons are classified according to four security levels, ranging from minimum custody (Level I) to maximum custody (Level IV). The vast majority of institutions are level III; however, most institutions are designed for a variety of security levels. For example, California Correctional Institution in Tehachapi has custody classifications of I, II, III and IV as do the women's facilities at Chino and Chowchilla. General differences between minimum and maximum security institutions in California are:

LEVEL I (Minimum Custody): Generally, inmates are housed in "open dormitories" and on grounds that are not secured by walls or fences. Inmates assigned to this classification level are non-violent, and they are usually serving less than 30 months. The majority (31%) of all CDC male inmates are housed in Level I facilities.[167]

LEVEL II (Light Medium): These inmates are assigned to dormitory-style housing, yet are confined by fences and are secured by armed officers within towers and ground posts. Inmates who have prior offenses, but are without a history of institutional violence or escapes, are typically housed at this custody level. About 24% of all CDC male inmates are housed in Level II facilities.[168]

LEVEL III (Medium): At this level, inmates are housed within cells rather than dormitories. The perimeter of their living area is walled, fenced and secured by armed officers. They generally serve longer sentences than inmates classified as Level I's or II's. The Level III inmate usually has served prior prison terms and has a history of serious behavioral problems while under institutional confinement. About 25% of the CDC's male inmate population are classified at Level III.[169]

LEVEL IV (Maximum): Inmates who have the most serious histories of crime and violence, and who are classified as considerable escape risks, are classified as Level IV (and are housed in the most secure facilities.) These prisoners reside in areas with fenced or walled perimeters, electronic security and armed officers both inside and outside of their living area. All Level IV inmates are confined to cells and permitted to engage only in a limited range of activities. The most secure Level IV units are known as a "SHU" (Security Housing Unit). The smallest segment of the CDC's adult male population (18%) is classified as Level IV.[170]

3. Serving Time

Prison Programs for California Inmates

After classification has been completed, new inmates are assigned and transported to the institution where they will be permanently housed. The inmate is then given a brief orientation to the institution, its rules and its staff. Inmates not assigned to SHU units or maximum custody will begin "programming." That is, they will spend a majority of their time engaging in many of the following structured activities:

MANUFACTURING: Inmates manufacture all of the clothes that they wear. This includes shoes, jackets and other apparel. Some of the clothes worn by state workers, such as safety vests for Cal Trans, are also made by inmates. They also make furniture and other products (flags, fabricated metal, concrete, printed materials) used in their institutions as well as within other state institutions, buildings and universities. Road signs are manufactured by inmates and Folsom Prison maintains a license plate factory. Much of the manufacturing carried out in prison is performed under the guidance of The P.I.A. (Prison Industry Authority). The P.I.A. is a private corporation, operated in conjunction with the CDC, that runs the factories, dairies laundries, farms and other service industries within a prison. The P.I.A.'s gross annual sales are in excess of $100 million.[171]

COMMUNITY SERVICE: Inmates assist communities near prisons by maintaining parks and roads, restoring community buildings, or making toys for needy children. Trained inmate firefighters protect California's forests and wildlands.

VOCATIONAL TRAINING: There are more than 65 specific skills and trades programs offered to inmates by the CDC. Included among these are automotive repair, electronics, woodworking, building and metal trades, machinery repair, masonry, meatcutting and horse training.

INSTITUTIONAL SUPPORT: Inmates are used to assist institutional staff in the day-to-day operations and maintenance of prisons. Specifically, inmates serve as clerical assistants, cooks, gardeners, hospital orderlies and in a variety of other support capacities.

ACADEMIC CLASSES: The largest primary and secondary adult education program in California is offered by the CDC. Inmates within each institution can complete their elementary and secondary diplomas, including English as a second language). More advanced college-level coursework is also offered on a limited basis.

4. A Day in the Life of a California Inmate

The Typical Daily Schedule of an Inmate:

5:00 am: Inmates counted
6:00 am: General population wakes up (kitchen workers awake at 4:00am)
6:15 am: Breakfast
6:45 am: Prisoners on medication line up for pills
7:00 am: Report to work or classes
9:15 am: Cells unlocked for prisoners without programs, go to exercise yard
11:00 am: Yard Ends. Inmates return to cells
11:30 am: Lunch (in sack)
12:00 pm: High security inmates counted
2:00 pm: Work day ends for inmates with jobs in Prison Authority
2:30 pm: Cells unlocked, prisoners return to yard, dayrooms
3:30 pm: Classes end for inmates in education or job training
3:45 pm: Inmates return from yard, cells locked
4:30 pm: Mail distributed, inmates counted
5:00 pm: Dinner
6:30 pm: Cells unlocked inmates return to yard or dayrooms
9:30 pm: Inmates returned to cells
12:00 am: Final count of inmates

Items Which Inmates are Allowed to Have:

o Clothes: Denim jeans, blue work shirt, leather work shoes
o Canteen: Cigarettes, soda, vitamins, candy, ice cream, canned foods, personal care products, stationary, pens.
o Catalogue: Mail order firms specialize in sales to inmates in correctional facilities, approved clocks, small televisions, radios, tape players, earphones, approved clothing and personal care items.
o Equipment: Guitar, typewriter, no more than two plug-in appliances
o Reading: Law books, general interest books, magazines
o Cable TV: Reception is poor in most prisons, so the state provides cable TV. Prisons rent and broadcast movies via cable to inmates' cells.
o Exercise: Weights, softball, soccer, handball, basketball, track, bags for boxing

The Typical Inmate Diet:

Breakfast: Stewed fruit, hot cereal, scrambled eggs, turkey-ham, muffin w/butter, coffee, milk
Lunch: Turkey, baloney, cheese sand., apple, chips, cookies, beverage
Dinner: Salad, beef stew w/noodles, canned peas, roll, butter, cake, beverage[172]

5. "Good Time" Credit

Although California's determinate sentencing laws require that convicted offenders serve a prison term that has been fixed by the Legislature, inmates may obtain early release through "good time" credit. However, the amount of good time inmates can earn is determined by the nature of their offense and by their willingness to participate in educational or training programs. This is called the "Work Incentive Program."[173]

With the exception of violent offenders, who must serve at least 85% of their original term, it is possible for inmates serving non life sentences to reduce their prison time by one-half. This is called the "one-for-one" plan. That is, inmates who participate in the Work Incentive Program will be given one day of good time credit for every day they successfully participate in either education or training classes.[174]

Inmates who do not participate in the Work Incentive Program are given good time credit for "good" institutional behavior (i.e., following orders, not fighting). However, these inmates are on the "two-for-one" plan and are given one day of good time credit for every two days of "good" behavior. Therefore, it is possible for these inmates to reduce their prison term by one-third.[175]

Because inmates serving some life terms (such as "three strikers" who are not LWOP's: Life Without the Possibility of Parole) receive an indeterminate sentence, they too can be granted early release. Their date of release, however, is determined by a special independent agency called the Board of Prison Terms (BPT). The majority of cases coming before the BPT include those sentenced for murder, attempted murder, kidnap for robbery or ransom, sex offenders and habitual felons. The BPT has a 93% denial rate for parole requests.[176]

In general, good time credits can be taken away as well. They can also be given back once taken away. However, considering that the average inmate's original sentence is 42.8 months and the average time served in the CDC is 21.1 months, nearly all inmates who are eligible to achieve the maximum number of good time credit while in custody appear to do so.[177]

6. Release and Parole

Parole is automatically given to inmates upon their release back into society. The newly released inmates are given one set of civilian clothing, a small sum of money ($200) and are told to report immediately to their parole agent. Then the inmate must return to the county where he or she was originally sentenced, unless their is sufficient cause to place the inmate elsewhere (this occurs in roughly one out of every ten cases). Inmates without a place to live will reside in a state sponsored halfway house or shelter while re-establishing roots in the community.[178]

7. Final Release and Parole

After inmates have successfully completed parole they are no longer under the authority of the CDC. The amount of time spent on parole depends on the crime and the parolee's institutional behavior. Most parolees serve between one and three years on parole, with most being discharged after one year without any violations. Those with life sentences who are paroled spend three to five years on parole, with most being discharged after their third year without any violations.[179]

Those inmates who do not meet the conditions of their parole are sent back to custody for up to one year. An addition 12 months can be added to the inmate's revocation term for engaging in misconduct while in custody. Non-violent offenders are often sent to a Return To Custody (RTC) Center where they are confined to facility grounds during their revocation period. RTC's are small community-based facilities designed to help reduce prison overcrowding.

CONSERVATION CAMPS: "PRISONS WITHOUT WALLS"

Approximately 4,000 male and female inmates serve their time in conservation camps rather than in institutions. Most of California's conservation camp system is operated by the CDC in conjunction with the California Department of Forestry and Fire Protection. Some camps in Southern California are operated jointly with the Los Angeles County Fire Department.[180]

Typically, assignment to a conservation camp is a difficult task for an inmate. First, inmates must be classified as a minimum security risk. Second, they must be physically fit and have no history of violent offending, kidnapping, sex crimes, arson or escape. The average sentence for an inmate serving his or her time in camp is two years.[181]

Once assigned to camp, inmates first complete two weeks of physical conditioning and then complete a second two weeks of training in fire fighting techniques. While inmates are in training, their progress in constantly reviewed by CDC staff. Inmates who do not make satisfactory progress during the training phase are returned to a CDC institution.[182]

Between 60 to 120 inmates occupy each camp. There are 38 camps located throughout the entire state. Inmates live in military-style barracks and are not confined by gun towers or security fences. However, there have been very few escapes from camps because camp inmates are usually close to the end of their sentences.[183]

Aside from fighting fires, camp inmates perform a variety of services to the public. These include graffiti removal, flood control, wildlife habitat preservation, reforestation, trash clean-ups and park maintenance. The pay received for work, including fire fighting, is about $1.00 per day.[184]

EXPERIMENTAL PRISONS: "BOOT CAMPS"

California, like may other states, is currently exploring the idea of correctional confinement of inmates in military-style "boot camps." The project's title is Alternative Sentencing Program (ASP). The state's first experimental camp was located at San Quentin in the early 1990s. Inmates eligible for the program are those having committed non-violent offenses (mainly property crimes) who are 40 years or younger and have not served a prior state or federal prison term.

The entire "boot camp" program lasts for ten months. The first phase of the program, which lasts for four months, involves rigorous physical activity, military drills, structured work and counseling. The second phase is an assignment to a specialized work furlough facility for 60 days, where the inmates perform closely supervised activities under a less rigid "drill camp" atmosphere. Last, the inmate is given intensive parole which stresses employment, schooling and training for 120 days. Inmates who fail to complete any or all stages of the "boot camp" training are sent back to serve their time in a state prison facility.[185]

Pictured above: A typical inmate reception center where "classification" takes place.

3.4

THE CALIFORNIA YOUTH AUTHORITY

THE BEGINNING OF STATE YOUTH CORRECTIONS

When California became a state in 1850, separate correctional facilities for adult and juveniles were not available. During these early years of statehood, serious juvenile delinquents were committed to either San Quentin or Folsom (along with adult offenders).[186]

From 1850 to 1890, various small reform schools for delinquent children and adolescents were founded in the San Francisco area. However, in 1890, the Legislature enacted law establishing the first two major state institutions for juvenile delinquents: The Whittier State Reformatory (now Fred C. Nelles School in Whittier) and the Preston School of Industry (in Ione, Amador County). The Whittier State Reformatory opened in 1891 with an enrollment of 300 male and female youths. The Preston School opened in 1892. During this period, however, some wards were still being confined with adults at San Quentin.[187]

Many events took place during the first decade of the 1900's that would eventually shape today's juvenile justice system in California. For example, in 1903, the Legislature enacted law establishing separate juvenile courts. By 1909, juvenile hall were being established in nearly every county. In 1913, all female wards were transferred from Whittier to the state's first all female juvenile facility: The Ventura School for Girls.[188]

THE CREATION OF THE CALIFORNIA YOUTH AUTHORITY

The California Youth Authority (CYA) was formally established in 1941, which marked the beginning of a new era where juvenile corrections became totally separate from adult corrections. The new CYA, under its first Director Karl Holton, was comprised of the existing Preston, Nelles and Ventura institutions. Various camps and a delinquency prevention unit were also created under the CYA's administration. In 1945, a separate division of juvenile parole was also established.[189]

CYA INSTITUTIONS

Today's CYA is the nation's largest and most complex system of juvenile corrections. It provides institutional training and parole supervision for juvenile and young adult offenders. Presently, the CYA supervises over 9,000 youths in its institutions and camps and another 6,000 on parole. The CYA operates eleven institutions and four camps and 17 parole offices.[190]

The primary role of the CYA is public safety and "rehabilitation" of the youthful offender (in contrast to the CDC's mission of "punishment"). For males, there are two CYA reception centers: The Northern Reception Center in Sacramento and the Southern Reception Center in Norwalk. All women are received at the Ventura School in Ventura (which is now co-educational and houses males as well).

On average, each CYA institution has approximately 550 beds. However, the largest of CYA's institutions is the Heman G. Stark Youth Training School located in the City of Chino. There, some 2,000 young men receive extensive vocational training. The CYA's second largest institution is the Preston School located in Ione. Interestingly, the Preston School was the site of the nation's first "boot camp" style juvenile correctional program known as "LEAD" (Leadership, Esteem, Ability, Discipline). LEAD involves a four-month intensive training, treatment and education program based on the military model (in cooperation with the California National Guard), which is followed by six months of intensive parole supervision.[191]

All institutions have treatment programs for drug and alcohol abusers. In particular the Karl Holton Drug and Alcohol Abuse Treatment Center located in Stockton houses high risk substance abusing males. Special programs for sex offenders are offered at the O.H. Close Center in Stockton and the Fred C. Nelles School in Whittier. Also, a large number of the CYA population spends some of their commitment time in conservation camps. Fighting fires and performing public service are the primary activities at these camps.[192]

CYA OFFENDER POPULATION

The majority (85%) of CYA's population consists of youths and adolescents who have committed serious crimes while under the age of 18. The other 15% of the inmate population is made up of adult law breakers (over the age of 18) that have, for various reasons, been committed to the CYA. Most offenders housed at CYA are between the ages of 15-22, with very few in the 13 or younger age bracket. The average first age of commitment at the time of admission to the CYA is 17.5 years. No one in the CYA is over 25 years old.[193]

The largest number of CYA commitments came from Los Angeles County (36%), followed by Northern California (27%), the San Francisco Bay Area (19%) and Southern California, excluding Los Angeles County (18%). Violent offenders comprise 59% of the overall population. Property and drug offenders make up an additional 27% and 8%, respectively. The predominate ethnicity of the CYA population is Hispanic (47%), followed by African-American (29%), Caucasian (15%) and Asian (6%). One out of every four youth committed to the CYA have no prior convictions or commitments.[194]

THE CYA PROCESS

1. Commitment:

There are basically three ways an offender is committed to the CYA:

- o Directly by a juvenile court;
- o Tried as an adult and committed by a criminal court;
- o Tried as an adult and committed to the California Department of Corrections (CDC) but ordered to be housed in a CYA facility.

2. Doing Time:

While younger offenders attend school most of the day, older offenders usually attend school part-time and spend the remainder of their time in vocational training. Like adult inmates, offenders in the CYA work assigned jobs within the institution such as grounds maintenance or food preparation. Some jobs pay about $1.00 per day, which can be used to help pay victim restitution costs. Offenders are also assigned a counselor, and some are provided psychiatric or psychological assistance. Those assigned to conservation camps learn valuable fire fighting skills and are called upon to fight fires throughout the state should the need arise.[195]

3. Release:

CYA Commitments from juvenile court. Unlike sentencing for adults, CYA commitments are indeterminate in nature. This means that there are no fixed terms or "flat time" granted for specific offenses. The specific period of incarceration in CYA is typically determined by the severity of the offender's offense and the offender's ability to successfully complete specific program goals. The offender's ultimate release from the CYA is determined by the Youthful Offender Parole Board. However, California law stipulates that the term of incarceration imposed on offenders committed to the CYA cannot exceed the limits of determinate sentences for adults committing the same crime. In addition, for those youths committed directly from juvenile court to the CYA, the CYA's jurisdiction ends on the offender's 25th birthday. It must be noted that offenders **committed directly to the CYA by juvenile court** are not merely transferred to the adult Department of Corrections; they are released.

Adult Offenders Committed to the CYA. Release procedures for adult offenders committed to the CYA under special circumstances are different from discussed above. Adult offenders housed in the CYA are usually released to parole automatically when their fixed sentence has been completed. If the adult offender was originally committed to the CDC (adult prison) but ordered to the CYA, he or she **may** be transferred to the Department of Corrections on or before their 25th birthday.

4. Parole:

The CYA operates 17 parole offices in its Northern and Southern Regions. All parole decisions fall under the general administration of the Youthful Offender Parole Board (YOPB). The YOPB is a separate administrative agency which is similar in function to the CDC's Board of Prison Terms. Parole agents work under the administration of the Parole Services and Community Corrections branch of the CYA.

CYA parole agents provide newly released offenders with a range of services including resident placement, family counseling, job development and placement as well as school enrollment. During the first 90 days of the offender's release, he or she is intensively supervised by a parole agent. Parole agents conduct approximately 689,000 drug tests annually and maintain a close watch on offenders in the community. Those who successfully complete their parole earn an "honorable discharge" from the CYA.[196]

GETTING PROBATION IN CALIFORNIA

By law, each of California's 58 counties maintains a probation department for both adults and juveniles. The chief administrator of probation services in each county holds the title of Probation Officer of the County (commonly referred to as the Chief Probation Officer). It is the duty of the Chief Probation Officer to appoint deputies (i.e., Deputy Probation Officers) to carry out the day-to-day administration of adult and juvenile probation services. Like all other branches of the criminal justice system the state, probation departments in many California counties are among the largest in the nation.

THE JUVENILE PROBATION PROCESS

1. Referral: Referrals can either be "in-custody" or "non-custody." The majority of referrals are "in-custody" resulting from an arrest made by police. Parents or schools reporting delinquent activity to probation officials would be an example of a "non-custody" referral.

   Juveniles who violate the law in California are known as a "602" (corresponding to the California Welfare and Institutions Code). Status offenders, e.g., beyond parental control or truancy, are referred to as a "601."

2. Intake: In California, the person who brings the minor to the attention of the probation department (i.e., police, parents, school) signs a document known as an "Application for Petition." This document describes the minor's alleged legal/status offense. A probation officer known as an "Intake Officer" will then conduct an investigation of the circumstances surrounding the minor's arrest. Following the investigation, the probation officer may:
   - o dismiss the case
   - o counsel and release the minor
   - o initiate informal probation (usually six months)
   - o request the District Attorney to prosecute

3. Petition: If the decision is to prosecute, a "Petition" is filed against the minor (i.e., a document officially "charging" the youth with the alleged offense). Further investigation into the background of the case will be undertaken by the probation department.

4. Hearing: The case is heard in juvenile court and "disposed of" within a short period after the petition is filed (usually within 15 days). Further investigations are conducted. These include gathering information about the alleged offense, the minor's family background, the victim, the minor's prior criminal activity and so forth. If the minor is found by the court to be "involved" (i.e., guilt as charged), results of further probation investigations containing recommendations for sanctioning the minor are forwarded to the sentencing juvenile judge or commissioner (e.g., probation supervision or commitment to the California Youth Authority).

5. Transfer: In very special circumstances, the California Penal Code stipulates that minors between the ages of 14-17 charged with one or more serious felonies can be "transferred" to stand trial in adult court. When this is the case, probation officers will perform special investigations to determine whether remedies provided by California's juvenile justice system are suitable for the minor. If they are not deemed suitable, the minor will be recommended to be moved into the adult criminal justice system.[197]

THE ADULT PROBATION SYSTEM

Whereas juveniles who commit serious as well as minor crimes are processed through California's county probation system, adult probationers tend to be minor and/or first-time offenders. For adults, probation is one of many sanctions that can be used alone or in combination with other sanctions. Many adults who spend time on probation may also be required to serve jail time or participate in programs such as substance abuse counseling, vocational job training or psychiatric treatment. Perhaps the most critical function of "adult" probation officers in California, along with client supervision, is their service as an investigator to Superior and Municipal Courts. Specifically, these officers often prepare many reports that are used by courts to make critical decisions regarding the handling of a defendant. For example, probation officers routinely submit "pre-sentence investigation" reports to the court regarding defendants who are awaiting a judgement of guilt or innocence. This report contains information such as details regarding the offense, statements from the crime victims and other persons involved in the case as well as the offender's social and demographic background. For those defendants who have been found guilty, the probation officer often presents the court with a "sentencing report." This document contains the probation officer's recommendation to the sentencing judge for an appropriate sanction for the defendant (for example, the granting of probation or incarceration).[198]

THE CALIFORNIA PROBATION OFFICER

Probation officers in California are sworn peace officers. However, the peace officer functions of a probation officer are distinctly different than those of a police officer. According to Penal Code 830.5, which outlines the peace officer status of correctional, parole and probation officers, arrest powers of these officers are limited "....to conditions of parole or probation by any person in state or parole or probation or violations during the course of employment." Probation officers may carry firearms, provided that they have completed the appropriate training and certification. Today, many California probation officers who work high risk assignments in specialized units or with high risk clients do carry firearms.

ON THE CUTTING EDGE OF CALIFORNIA PROBATION

Intensive Supervision and "The Team Approach"

Most probation supervision in California is known as "general supervision"; that is, the probation officer maintains minimal contact with the client (usually once per month, or longer). For special categories of clients, "intensive supervision" is used. These clients include gang members, repeat drug offenders and other high risk probationers. The typical intensive supervision caseload is 15 clients per probation officer. The Orange County Probation Department has pioneered a special "team approach" to intensive supervision known as the TARGET Program. In this program, dangerous street gang members who have been granted probation are intensively supervised by a team consisting of a county probation officer, a local police officer and a deputy district attorney. Close watch is kept on the probationer so when (or if) a legal or technical violation is observed, the coordinated effort between probation, prosecution and the police results in a quick and effective solution to the case.[199]

<u>The Eight Percent Solution</u>

Another innovative program explored by the Orange County Probation Department is the "Eight Percent Solution." This program has served as a model for probation agencies throughout the nation. The program is based on habitual offending research that has pointed out that a relatively small proportion of offenders (in Orange County's case, "eight percent") are responsible for a large proportion of crime. In a seven-year study of thousands of youth place on probation, the Orange County Probation Department discovered that about 70% of first-time offenders were never arrested again. About 8% became habitual offenders responsible for more than half of the repeat appearances in the juvenile system. The probation department studies the critical "8%" and developed a profile to identify them and focus their attention on providing special treatment for these clients. Warning signs of the "8%" include:

- o 15 or younger at the time of the first offense
- o problems in school
- o problems at home
- o history of drug and/or alcohol abuse
- o patterns of delinquent behavior (gangs, run aways, stealing)[200]

THE FUTURE OF CALIFORNIA PROBATION

As a direct result of tax cutbacks such as Proposition 13, probation services to adults and juveniles in California have been steadily shrinking. It not uncommon to find probation officers in some counties that have caseloads of more than 300 clients. Such high caseloads, along with dwindling resources and staff, have caused many of California's probation departments to keep tabs on their clients via mail rather than by personal contact. However, new technology such as electronic monitoring and house arrest have offered some relief to the California probation officer's excessive workload. Some California probation departments have also started volunteer probation officer programs to help ease growing officer to client caseloads.

Although probation serves a vital function in California's system of justice, many critics argue that probationers have high recidivism rates and that probation amounts to "doing nothing at all." In a widely cited 1985 study of California probationers conducted by the Rand Corporation, it was found that more than half of adult felons on probation were convicted of new crimes within 40 months and that one-third of those were returned to probation. However, regardless of criticisms aimed at the treatment capacity of the state's probation system, probation will continue to serve a vital support function to California's courts throughout the immediate and distant future.

3.6

THE END: CALIFORNIA'S DEATH ROW

CONDEMNED PRISONERS

In California, executions in the name of the state were first authorized in 1851. Death by hanging was the method of choice. Gallows were located at both San Quentin and Folsom prisons. The first state execution was carried out in 1893. However, the last state hanging was held on May 1, 1942 at Folsom. After 1942, hanging was outlawed due to strong public opinions criticizing the method for being excessively gruesome and inhumane. A total of 307 male inmates have been hanged in California, 215 at San Quentin and 92 at Folsom.

Offenders sentenced to die in California after August 1937 were executed by means of lethal gas rather than the gallows. The "gas chamber" was originally installed (and remains to this day) at San Quentin. It was first used in 1938 for the double execution of Robert Cannon and Albert Kessell, who killed a prison warden in a foiled escape attempt. A total of 191 inmates (including 4 females) have been executed in California's gas chamber.

California is only one of a handful of states that uses lethal gas as a primary method of execution. Most states use lethal injection. Many prison officials feel that the gas chamber is better than other methods because it allows considerable physical distance between the condemned inmate and staff members who must perform the execution (lethal injection requires the probing of veins and electrocution requires that the inmate's head be shaved). Opponents of the gas chamber argue that it is "cruel and unusual" punishment because death by asphyxiation takes about 10 minutes.[201]

The debate over the constitutionality of the California's gas chamber reached a peak during the execution of Robert Alton Harris in 1992. Harris was convicted in 1978 of the brutal slaying of two San Diego teenagers. He and defense attorneys on his behalf argued that his execution by lethal gas was "cruel and unusual" punishment and a violation of the U.S. Constitution's Eighth Amendment. Based on the argument, the Ninth Circuit Court of Appeals granted Harris a reprieve just seconds after he was strapped in the gas chamber and awaiting the Warden's signal for his execution. However, the U.S. Supreme Court upheld California's right to carry out the death penalty by lethal gas. Just two hours after Harris was granted his reprieve, he was returned to the gas chamber and executed.

As a direct result of the legal questions brought about by the Harris execution, it is now law in California that a condemned inmate may choose between lethal injection or lethal gas. The purpose of this law is to stop last-minute appeals by prisoners who argue that death by lethal gas is unconstitutional. California has carried out two executions (Robert Alton Harris, 1992 and David Edwin Mason, 1993) since 1967.[202]

CONDEMNED WOMEN

It is interesting to note that California has one of the nation's largest condemned women prisoner populations. Four women have been put to death since 1893. Each has been a convicted murderer and has died in the gas chamber.

The first woman to be put to death was Juanita Spinelli in 1941. Spinelli, nicknamed "The Dutchess," was a San Francisco crime leader who was convicted of killing a gang member to prevent him from talking to authorities about her criminal affairs. She was also an "ex wrestler" and a professional knife thrower. Perhaps the most famous of California's condemned women was Barbara Graham, who was executed in 1955. A major motion picture was produced about Graham's alleged robbery and murder of a wealthy Burbank woman.

Women sentenced to death are not housed at San Quentin's "death row," but rather are housed at the Central Women's Facility in Chowchilla. Those who are executed are driven to San Quentin, where they spend their final hours.[203]

NOTES/REFERENCES

1. John P. Kenney, The California Police (Springfield, IL: Charles C. Thomas Publishers, 1964), p. 21.

2. Samuel Walker, The Police in America: An Introduction (New York: McGraw-Hill, Inc., 1992), p. 19.

3. Charles R. Swanson, Leonard Territo, and Robert W. Taylor, Police Administration: Structures, Processes, and Behavior (New York: Macmillan Publishing Company, 1993), p. 4.

4. Philip John Stead, Pioneers in Policing (Montclair, NJ: Patterson Smith Publishing Corporation, 1977), pp. 181-182.

5. Neal E. Troutman, Law Enforcement Training (Springfield, IL: Charles C. Thomas Publishers, 1986), p.4.

6. Stead, Pioneers in Policing, p. 183.

7. William E. Caldwell, "LEEP-Its Development and Potential," Police Chief, August 1970, p. 24.

8. Jack L. Kuykendall, "Toward an Integrated Professional Model of Administration of Justice Education," Journal of California Law Enforcement 10, (January 1976): 103.

9. Stead, Pioneers in Policing, p. 184.

10. National Institute of Law Enforcement and Criminal Justice, The National Manpower Survey of the Criminal Justice System 5 (Washington, D.C.: U.S. Department of Justice, 1980), p. 45.

11. Stead, Pioneers in Policing, pp. 185-187.

12. Walker, The Police in America: An Introduction, p. 17.

13. Stead, Pioneers in Policing, pp. 207-219.

14. Walker, The Police in America: An Introduction, p. 18.

15. Swanson, Territo, and Taylor, Police Administration: Structures, Processes, and Behavior, p. 249.

16. Kenney, The California Police, p. 81.

17. Swanson, Territo, and Taylor, Police Administration: Structures, Processes and Behavior, p. 249.

18. Edward A. Farris, "Five Decades of American Policing, 1932-1982: The Path to Professionalism," Police Chief, November 1982, p. 31.

19. National Advisory Commission on Criminal Justice Standards and Goals, Police (Washington, D.C.: U.S. Department of Justice, 1973), pp. vii-x.

20. Kenney, The California Police, p. 107.

21. Ibid., p. 18.

22. Ibid., p. 19.

23 Ibid.

24. Law Enforcement Division, Office of Emergency Services, Law Enforcement Mutual Aid Plan (Sacramento, CA: Office of Emergency Services, 1994), p. 31.

25. California Commission on Peace Officer Standards and Training, Employment Data for California Law Enforcement, 1992/1993 (Sacramento, CA: California Commission on Peace Officer Standards and Training, 1994), p. 27.

26. Federal Bureau of Investigation, 1993 Uniform Crime Reports (Washington, D.C.: U.S. Government Printing Office, 1994), p. 295.

27. California Commission on Peace Officer Standards and Training, Employment Date for California Law Enforcement, 1992/1993, p. 27.

28. California Department of Justice, 1991-1992 Biennial Report Sacramento, CA: California Department of Justice, 1993), pp. 21-51.

29. Law Enforcement Division, Office of Emergency Services, Law Enforcement Mutual Aid Plan, pp. 13-21.

30. Frank Schmalleger, Criminal Justice Today (Englewood Cliffs, NJ: Regents/Prentice Hall, 1993), p. 158.

31. Michael Sgobba, "Marshals of California," Journal of California Law Enforcement 17, (Summer 1983): 113.

32. Walker, The Police in America: An Introduction, pp.42-43.

33. Ibid., p. 42.

34. Ibid., p. 47.

35. California Commission on Peace Officer Standards and Training, Employment Data for California Law Enforcement, 1993-1993, p. 22.

36. Robert J. Meadows, Fundamentals of Protection and Safety for the Private Protection Officer, (Englewood Cliffs, NJ: Prentice Hall, 1995), p. 7.

37. Pinkerton Security and Investigation Services, People and Technology: The Pinkerton Difference, (Encino, CA: Pinkerton Security and Investigation Services, 1995), p. 6.

38. Walker, The Police in America: An Introduction, p. 52.

39. Meadows, Fundamentals of Protection and Safety for the Private Protection Officer, p. 9.

40. Pinkerton Security and Investigation Services, People and Technology: The Pinkerton Difference, p. 6.

41. Schmalleger, Criminal Justice Today, p. 173.

42. Schmalleger, Criminal Justice Today p. 177.

43. George L. Kelling and Mark H. Moore, "The Evolving Strategy of Policing," Perspectives on Policing 4, (November 1988): 2-4.

44. Arthur W. Sjoquist, Los Angeles Police Department Commemorative Book: 1869-1984 (Los Angeles: Los Angeles Police Revolver and Athletic Club, Inc., 1984), p. 56.

45. James Q. Wilson, Varieties of Police Behavior: The Management of Law and Order in Eight Communities (Cambridge, MA: Harvard University Press, 1968).

46. Schmalleger, Criminal Justice Today, pp. 177-178.

47. George L. Kelling and Mark H. Moore, Perspectives on Policing, pp. 4-6.

48. Arthur W. Sjoquist, Los Angeles Police Department Commemorative Book: 1869-1984, pp. 62-65.

49. Ibid. pp.89-119.

50. National Advisory Commission on Criminal Justice Standards and Goals, Report on Police (Washington, D.C.: U.S. Government Printing Office, 1973), pp. v-x.

51. Schmalleger, Criminal Justice Today, p. 178.

52. Robert Trojanowicz and Bonnie Bucqueroux, Community Policing: How to Get Started

(Cincinnati: Anderson Publishing Co., 1994), p. 2.

53. Kelling and Moore, Perspectives on Policing, p. 10.

54. Trojanowicz and Bucqueroux, Community Policing: How to Get Started, p. vii.

55. California Department of Justice, Biennial Report of Major Activities: 1991-1992 (Sacramento, CA: California Department of Justice, 1993), p. xviii.

56. Dennis P. Rosenbaum, The Challenge of Community Policing: Testing the Promises (Thousand Oaks, CA: Sage Publications, 1994).

57. Schmalleger, Criminal Justice Today, p. 178.

58. California Specialized Training Institute, California Specialized Training Institute Catalog of Training Courses (Sacramento, CA: California Office of Emergency Services, 1994), p. 4.

59. Kenneth J. Peak, Justice Administration: Police Courts, and Corrections Management (Englewood Cliffs, NJ: Prentice Hall, 1995), p. 155.

60. Ibid. p. 155.

61. Robert M. Shusta, Multicultural Law Enforcement: Strategies for Peacekeeping in a Diverse Society (Englewood Cliffs, NJ: Prentice Hall, 1995), pp. 64 and 415-418.

62. S.H. Barnett, Police-Celebrity Golf Memorial Program (Los Angeles: Police Memorial Foundation, 1973), p. 86.

63. Walker, The Police in America: An Introduction, p. 161.

64. Glenn Levant, Drug Abuse Resistance Education (Los Angeles: DARE America, 1988), p. 3.

65. National Advisory Commission on Criminal Justice Standards and Goals, Report on Police, pp. 528-529.

66. Thomas E. Drabek and Gerard J. Hoetmer, Emergency Management: Principles and Practice for Local Government (Washington, D.C.: International City Management Association, 1991), p. 136.

67. Law Enforcement Division, Office of Emergency Services, Law Enforcement Guide for Emergency Operations Planning (Sacramento, CA: Office of Emergency Services, 1994), p. 15.

68. Los Angeles Times Staff, "Ten Costliest Catastrophic Events in U.S. History," Los Angeles Times, 21 May 1992, Section D. p.1.

69. Los Angeles Times Staff, 4:31 (Los Angeles: Los Angeles Times, 1994), p. 7.

70. Mark Gladstone and Richard Paddock, "Unabomber Package Sent to UC," Los Angeles Times, 3 July 1995, Section A, p. 1.

71. William L. Tafoya, "The Future of Law Enforcement? A Chronology of Events," Criminal Justice International (May/June 1991): 4.

72. Frank J. Schober, "The California Earthquake: Now is the Time to be Ready," Journal of California Law Enforcement 16 (Summer 1982): 155.

73. Law Enforcement Division, Office of Emergency Services, Law Enforcement Mutual Aid Plan (Sacramento, CA: Office of Emergency Services, 1994). p. 2.

74. Law Enforcement Division, Office of Emergency Services, Law Enforcement Guide for Emergency Operations Planning, p. 2.

75. Ibid. p. 54.

76. Ibid. p. 17.

77. Woodrow Williams, "Law Enforcement in the 1990s and Beyond: A Challenge for All Californians," Journal of California Law Enforcement 28 (1994): 29.

78. Ibid., p. 32.

79. Gregory R. Berg, "The Future of Community Policing in Large California Police Departments," Journal of California Law Enforcement 28 (1994): 72-77.

80. Williams, Journal of California Law Enforcement, pp. 30-34.

81. Kenneth J. Peak, Justice Administration: Police, Courts, and Corrections Management (Englewood Cliffs, NJ: Prentice Hall, 1995), p. 138.

82. Anonymous, West's California Codes (St Paul, MN: West Publishing Co., 1995), p. 352.

83. Independent Commission on the Los Angeles Police Department, Report on the Independent Commission on the Los Angeles Police Department (Los Angeles: R.R. Donnelley Financial International Printing Services, 1991), p. 26.

84. Los Angeles Police Department, Use of Force Handbook (Los Angeles: Los Angeles Police Department Printing Services, 1995), pp. 2-23.

85. Ibid., p.15.

86. Schmalleger, Criminal Justice Today, p. 204.

87. Peak, Justice Administration: Police, Courts, and Corrections Management, p. 154.

88. Ed Bond, "Putting the Brakes on Hot Pursuit," Los Angeles Times, 11 July 1995, Section B, p. 3.

89. California Department of Motor Vehicles, California Vehicle Code (Sacramento, CA: California Department of Motor Vehicles, 1995), p. 592.

90. Los Angeles Police Department, Manual of the Los Angeles Police Department (Los Angeles: Los Angeles Police Department Printing Services, 1993), p. 108.

91. Geoffrey P. Alpert and Roger G. Dunham, Critical Issues in Policing (Prospect Heights, IL: Waveland Press, 1993), p. 523.

92. George T. Felkenes and Peter Charles Unsinger, Diversity, Affirmative Action and Law Enforcement (Springfield, IL: Charles C. Thomas, 1992), p. 22.

93. Cal. Civ. Proc. Code Sec. 43 (West 1995).

94. Cal. Const. art. 6, Sec. 8 (West 1995).

95. Cal. Const. art. 6, Sec. 16 (West 1995).

96. Cal. Gov't. Code Sec. 71143 (West 1995).

97. *See Generally,* Maria Dolan, *Rose Bird's Quest for Obscurity,* L.A. Times, Nov. 15, 1995, at A1.

98. *Riverside v. McLaughlin*, 111 S. Ct. 1661, 114 L.Ed.2d 49 (1991).

99. Cal. Penal Code Sec. 1268a (West 1995).

100. Cal. Penal Code Sec. 1305 (West 1995).

101. Prosecutorial discovery in California after *People v. Collie:* Need for legislation. (1983) 23 Santa Clara L.Rev.

102. *Small v. Transcontinental & Western Air,* (1950) 216 P.2d 36, 96 C.A.2d 408.

103. *See U.S. v. Smith,* 789 F.2d 196, cert. denied 479 U.S. 1017, 107 S.Ct. 668, 93 L.Ed.2d 720 (1986); *Stoneham v. U.S.,* 479 U.S. 1017, 107 S.Ct. 668, 93 L.Ed.2d 720 (1986).

104. Cal. Civ. Proc. Code Sub Sec. 194 (g), 198 (West 1995).

105. Cal. Trial Handbook 3d, V. 2 Sec. 31.1.

106. Witkin's Cal. Evidence 3d, Sub Sec. 588-592.

107. *See Cumminsky v. Superior Court,* (1992) 13 Ca. Rptr. 2d 551, 3 Cal.4th 1018, 839 P.2d 1059, modified, rehearding denied.

108. Cal. Civ. Proc. Code Sec. 2023 (West) 1995).

109. *See People v. Brown,* (App. 3 Dist. 1986), 223 Cal. Rptr. 66, 177 C.A. 3d 537.

110. *See Alvarado v. U.S.,* 497 U.S. 543, 110 S. Ct. 2995, 111 L.Ed 2d 439 (1990), on remand 923 F.2d 253, appeal after remand 951 F.2d 22.

111. *See generally, In re Lee,* (1918) 177 Cal.690, 171 pac. 958.

112. *See* discussion draft of sentencing guidelines and policy statements for organizations, 10 Whittier L.Rev. 7 (1988).

113. *See U.S. v. Chavez-Botello,* 905 F.2d 279 (9th Cir. 1990); *U.S. v. Michel,* 876 F.2d 784 (9th Cir. 1989).

114. Cal. Penal Code Sec. 190 et seq.

115. Cal. Penal Code Sec. 190.2.

116. *See generally, U.S. v. Brown,* 985 F. 2d 478 (9th Cir. 1993).

117. *See*, Juveniles in crimial courts, 23 U.C.L.A. Law Rev. 988 (1976); *In re Dennis J,* (1977) 140 Cal. Rptr. 463, 72 C.A. 3d 755.

118. *See People v. Robles,* (App. 5 Dist. 1994) 27 Cal. Rptr. 2d 196, 22 Cal. App. 4th 256, review granted and opinion superseded 29 Cal. Rptr.2d 152, 871 P.2d 204.

119. Cal. Penal Code Sec. 1002 et seq.

120. Cal. Penal Code Sec. 1203.01, 6220 et seq.

121. "California Street Terrorism Enforcement and Prevention Act" Added by Stats. 1988, c. 1242, Sec. 1, eff. Sept. 26, 1988, Stats. 1988, c. 1256, Sec. 1, eff Sept. 26 1988.

122. Cal. Penal Code Sec. 186.22 (a).

123. Cal. Penal Code Sec. 186 (e), (f).

124. Cal. Penal Code Sec. 667 (a) (4).

125. Cal. Penal Code Sec. 186.22 (e) (ii).

126. Origins and Impact: A Public Defender's Perspective, 23 Pac. L.J. 881 (1992).

127. Cal Health & Safety Code Sec. 25351 et seq.

128. *See generally,* Jocelyn Stewart, *Conviction is Country's First Unver Street Gang Law,* L.A. Times, July 4, 1990, at B4: U.S. Gives $1.3 Million for 3 Crime Task Forces, L.A. Times, March 28, 1995 at B2.

129. *See generally,* Jeanne F. Brooks, *Shaken Baby Death Stirs Outcry From Top Officials,* San Diego Union-Tribune, July 29, 1995, at B1.

130. Mary Floyd Williams, <u>History of the San Francisco Committee of Vigilance of 1851</u> (Berkeley, CA: University of California Press, 1921), pp. 44-45.

131. Ibid.

132. Sgt. Bob Fitzer, Personal interview conducted on June 30, 1995, San Francisco Police Department. (Sgt. Fitzer is regarded as the "unofficial" historian of the SFPD).

133. Williams, <u>History of the San Francisco Committee of Vigilance</u>, p. 45

134. Ibid.

135. Sourcebook of Criminal Justice Statistics 1994, see "Who's Who in Jail Management" (Washington, D.C.: U.S. Bureau of Justice Statistics, 1995), p. 171.

136. Ibid.

137. Sherman Block, <u>Training Manual: Los Angeles Sheriff's Dept.</u> (Los Angeles, CA: County of
Los Angeles, 1995), p. 27.

138. Ibid.

139. California Youth Authority, <u>Public Information Packet</u> (Sacramento, CA: California Youth Authority, 1995).

140. Ibid.

141. Los Angeles Times, Editorial: The Current State of Juvenile Hall (August 12, 1995), p. .7B

142. Ibid.

143. Williams, History of the San Francisco Committee of Vigilance of 1851, p. 48.

144. Ibid.

145. Michael D. Brown, The History of Chino Prison (Chino, CA: California Institution for Men, 1991), p. 32.

146. Ibid.

147. Ibid.

148. Ibid.

149. Ibid.

150. California Department of Corrections, Inside California Corrections (Videotape produced by California Department of Corrections, Office of Public Affairs, 1989).

151. Dan Morain, "A Precise Procedure for Killing," Los Angeles Times (April 11, 1992), p. 1A.

151. Brown, The History of Chino Prison, p. 64.

152. A.L. Voigt, A History of Correctional Administration in California from 1940 to Present (Unpublished Master's Thesis, University of California, Berkeley, 1948).

153. Ibid, pp. 43-49.

154. CDC, Inside California Corrections.

155. Voigt, A History of Correctional Administration, p. 104.

156. Ibid, p. 123.

157. California Department of Corrections, Correctional Facilities (Sacramento, CA: CDC, 1995).

158. California Department of Corrections, Prisons Without Walls (Sacramento, CA: CDC, 1995).

159. Dan Morain, "California's Profusion of Prisons," <u>Los Angeles Times</u> (October 16, 1994), p A1.

160. Ibid.

161. Ibid.

162. California Department of Corrections, <u>Fact Sheet</u> (Sacramento, CA: CDC, 1995).

163. California Department of Corrections, <u>Correctional Officer Employment Bulletin</u> (Sacramento, CA: CDC, 1995).

164. California Department of Corrections, <u>Corrections: Public Safety, Public Service</u> (Sacramento, CA: CDC, 1995).

165. Ibid.

166. Ibid.

167. Ibid.

168. Ibid.

169. Ibid.

170. Ibid.

171. Ibid.

172. John Hurst and Dan Morain, "California's Aging Prisons," <u>Los Angeles Times</u> (October 17, 1994).

173. California Department of Corrections, <u>Supervised Parole</u> (Sacramento, CA: CDC, 1995).

174. Personal interview with California Department of Corrections Parole Agent, Division IV Office, Pomona CA.

175. Ibid.

176. CDC, <u>Fact Sheet</u>.

177. Ibid.

178. CDC, <u>Supervised Parole</u>.

179. Ibid.

180. CDC, Prisons Without Walls.

181. Ibid.

182. Ibid.

183. Ibid.

184. Ibid

185. California Department of Corrections, Boot Camps (Sacramento, CA: CDC, 1995).

186. CYA, Public Information Packet.

187. Ibid.

188. Ibid.

189. Ibid.

190. Ibid.

191. Ibid.

192. Ibid.

193. Ibid.

194. Ibid.

195. Ibid.

196. Ibid.

197. Orange County Probation Department, Probation in Orange County (Santa Ana, CA: OCPD, 1995).

198. Rene Lynch, "O.C. Probation Has a Reputation for Success," Los Angeles Times (February 8, 1993).

199. Personal interview with DPO Randal Niznik, Orange County Probation Department.

200. Ibid.

201. Morain, A Precise Procedure for Killing.

202. Ibid.

203. Ibid.